Recent Themes in Historical Thinking

Historians in Conversation:
Recent Themes in Understanding the Past
Series editor, Louis A. Ferleger

Recent Themes in

HISTORICAL THINKING

Historians in Conversation

Edited by Donald A. Yerxa

THE UNIVERSITY OF SOUTH CAROLINA PRESS

© 2008 University of South Carolina

Published by the University of South Carolina Press
Columbia, South Carolina 29208

www.sc.edu/uscpress

Manufactured in the United States of America

17 16 15 14 13 12 11 10 09 08   10 9 8 7 6 5 4 3 2 1

Library of Congress Cataloging-in-Publication Data

Recent themes in historical thinking : historians in conversation / edited by Donald A. Yerxa.
    p. cm. — (Historians in conversation)
  Compiles articles that originally appeared in Historically speaking.
  Includes bibliographical references and index.
    ISBN 978-1-57003-740-5 (cloth : alk. paper) — ISBN 978-1-57003-741-2 (pbk :
alk. paper)
    1. History—Philosophy. 2. History—Methodology. I. Yerxa, Donald A., 1950–
II. Historical Society (Boston, Mass.). Historically speaking.
  D16.8.R3427 2008
  901—dc22   2007043177

This book was printed on Glatfelter Natures, a recycled paper with 50 percent postconsumer
waste content.

Contents

Series Editor's Preface

The Historical Society was founded in 1997 to create more venues for common conversations about the past. Consequently, in the autumn of 2001, the Historical Society launched a new type of publication. The society's president, George Huppert, and I believed that there was an important niche for a publication that would make the work of the most prominent historians more accessible to nonspecialists and general readers. We recruited two historians who shared this vision, Joseph S. Lucas and Donald A. Yerxa, and asked them to transform *Historically Speaking* into a journal of historical ideas. Up to that point, *Historically Speaking* had served as an in-house publication reporting on the society's activities and its members' professional accomplishments. Yerxa and Lucas quickly changed the layout and content of *Historically Speaking,* and within a short period of time many of the most prominent historians in the world began appearing in its pages—people such as Danielle Allen, Niall Ferguson, Daniel Walker Howe, Mary Lefkowitz, Pauline Maier, William McNeill, Geoffrey Parker, and Sanjay Subrahmanyam. *Historically Speaking*'s essays, forums, and interviews have drawn widespread attention. The *Chronicle of Higher Education*'s "Magazine and Journal Reader" section, for example, repeatedly has highlighted pieces appearing in *Historically Speaking.* And leading historians are loyal readers, praising *Historically Speaking* as a "must-read" journal, a "*New York Review of Books* for history," and "the most intellectually exciting publication in history that is currently available."

The Historical Society is pleased to partner with the University of South Carolina Press to publish a multivolume series, *Historians in Conversation: Recent Themes in Understanding the Past.* Each thematic volume pulls key essays, forums, and interviews from *Historically Speaking* and makes them accessible for classroom use and for the general reader. The original selections from *Historically Speaking* are supplemented with an introductory essay by Donald A. Yerxa along with suggestions for further reading.

Louis A. Ferleger

Acknowledgments

As editor of *Historically Speaking* since 2001, I have accumulated considerable debt to an amazingly talented and diverse group of scholars. This volume illustrates well the extent of my debt. It has been both a pleasure and an honor to work with them. It has also been my privilege to work with a terrific group of colleagues at the Historical Society: Louis Ferleger, Scott Hovey. Randall Stephens, and especially Joseph S. Lucas. Joe, my *Historically Speaking* coeditor, is a gifted historian and copy editor. His sharp mind and good humor have been utterly essential to the success of *Historically Speaking*.

Launching a new publication (or, more accurately in this case, radically transforming a fledgling one) always presents challenges. *Historically Speaking* would not exist in its present form had it not been for the vision, support, and timely encouragement of George Huppert.

Introduction

Historical Inquiry and Thinking Today

Donald A. Yerxa

Historical inquiry today is robust at multiple levels—from the topics historians explore to the approaches they use to find meaning and insight from the past. Historians are open to almost any aspect of human experience. The distinguished Oxford historian Sir Keith Thomas notes that historians now explore an astounding range of topics, "from childhood to old age, from dress to table manners, from smells to laughter, from sport to shopping, from barbed wire to masturbation."[1] A symptom of the expansiveness of historical inquiry is the increasing attention given to "the irrational, the eccentric and the bizarre"[2]—something that may also be fueled by the popularity of cultural history. Work in these topics also reveals that historians cultivate, as Thomas puts it, "a greater sense of the otherness of the past."[3]

Historians have become increasingly interested in looking at past human experience from the inside, the ways people experienced various things in their lives. What people thought happened and what it felt like may be more fascinating to historians than what "really happened."[4] Case in point: dismissing textual references to supernatural entities, such as angels or demons, as irrational, superstitious, or the result of some psychosocial phenomenon renders a version of the past that is too thin and does not come close to understanding how life was actually experienced. Indeed, this example suggests another significant trend in current historical inquiry: the movement away from explanation and causation to a search for meaning and understanding.[5]

Perhaps the most obvious trend in historical inquiry is the explosion of interest in history by the public at large. Although tenure committees seem to be slow to accept it, the gap between popular and academic history is narrowing. Some, like John Lukacs, vehemently deny that the distinction has any significance: there is simply good history and bad history.[6] Be that as it may, popular history is no longer only the domain of journalists and freelance writers; distinguished university historians are increasingly writing books for general readers and hosting television series. It is probably no coincidence that historians have also become more comfortable with inserting their own personal identity and voice into their work. The prominent British historian Richard J. Evans notes that those historians who become successful writers and/or television personalities are no longer anonymous scholars toiling away in archives and at their desks but are "bold and vivid characters purveying a particular interpretation and adopting a personal point of view." Old documentaries with archival footage, stills, and anonymous, authoritative voice-overs have given way to "sharply individualized [historian] presenters accompanying dramatic reconstructions and talking to the camera in real historical settings."[7]

An essentially upbeat assessment of historical inquiry such as this would have been almost unthinkable as recently as the mid-1990s. At that time many believed that history was under siege by postmodernist thinkers and their allies who threatened the very foundations of historical inquiry. In response many historians rushed to take up rhetorical arms against intellectual insurrectionists who under the banners of the linguistic turn and postmodernism set up barricades to overthrow established notions of historical epistemology and practice. Although it may be inaccurate to use the term *history wars* as a blanket description for these contentious times, there is no denying that many considered the discipline of history to be in genuine crisis in the 1990s.

For those embracing postmodernist theory, conventional approaches to writing and thinking about history were hopelessly flawed. It is epistemologically naïve, they asserted, to assume that historians can employ detached empirical-research methods to arrive at narratives that reasonably correspond with the past. Historical facts don't speak for themselves; nor can historians claim to know the past as it actually was. History—especially the particular way that modernity carved up and made sense of the past—is a failed enterprise, and historians should recognize that all they produce are "possible narrative representations" of the past. No serious thinker denied that the past happened, but postmodernists challenged the notion that the past exists outside historians' constructions of it. Because the past necessarily reaches us in "configured, troped, emplotted, read, mythologized and ideologized" ways,[8] postmodernists argued that the venerable "noble dream" of truthful and detached historical interpretation must be replaced with the more modest goal of historical representation. History so conceived is essentially a literary endeavor in which the distinction between the historian and the object of the historian's study is collapsed.[9]

For postmodernist sympathizers all this was liberating. Conventional understandings of and approaches to the past need no longer constrain the creative historian. Not surprisingly, however, many historians were alarmed by these notions. Some were downright outraged. One agitated Australian historian wrote a polemic arguing that postmodernists and cultural relativists were killing the traditional practice of history.[10] Others, like Evans and several of the founders of the Historical Society, warned that the cultivation of detachment and self-criticism, along with scrupulous assessment of sources, was integral to good history and could not be jettisoned without serious consequences to the integrity of historical inquiry.[11]

The postmodern challenge to historical knowledge was not the only reason for the acute sense of crisis many felt in the 1990s for the discipline of history. Some argued that the trinity of race, class, and gender had become a conceptual and ideological straitjacket of intellectual conformity, and those disciplines that on the whole were resistant to these rubrics—diplomatic, military, intellectual, political, church, and economic history—were being marginalized in the profession.[12] These subdisciplines could become "respectable" only if its practitioners abandoned conventional approaches that privilege such things as power, ideas, and statesmanship and looked at the past through these prescribed lenses.

Looking back now, postmodernism's epistemological challenge, which once appeared so formidable, seems more like, in Felipe Fernández-Armesto's words, "a paper tiger of fearful asymmetry."[13] By and large, practicing historians have rejected the nihilistic tendencies of postmodernism in favor of a commonsensical approach to their craft.[14] They accept the constructed and literary nature of their work and the necessary reliance on conceptual frameworks and hermeneutical devices imported from the historian's present. But they do not lose sleep over epistemological matters or question the value of creating narratives based on reliable sources.

Fernández-Armesto has also noted, "As the tide receded, postmodernism left a rich residue on the shore encouraging historical beachcombing."[15] What is this residue? After postmodernism's critique of metanarratives (grand schemes employed to explain the past), historians on the whole are reluctant to conduct large-scale studies that explore change over long periods of time. They are much more comfortable with microhistories. Indeed, cultural history has emerged as one of the key subdisciplines.[16] Skittishness about grand narratives has also contributed to an emphasis on individuals in historical literature. "Historians began writing about people again," Evans contends, "and above all about humble, ordinary people, history's obscure, the losers and bystanders in the process of historical change."[17] Recent years have witnessed much more interest in historical biography and a larger role for human agency and historical contingency in historical narratives. Indeed, contingency (along with complexity) may be the core notion in the contemporary historian's functional philosophy of history. With contingency has also come growing interest in counterfactuals. If humans indeed shape history by their actions and ideas, then things might have been very different. Taken to an extreme, counterfactual analysis becomes sheer speculation, but employed with circumspection it provides added insight into the important choices people have made.

Not all these recent trends in historical thinking and practice are the direct result of postmodernism. Many have antecedents in the historiographical currents of the 1960s and 1970s. But much of historical thinking today has been influenced by postmodernist sensibilities. Neither, it should be added, are these trends universal; there are countervailing developments. Three examples will suffice: otherness versus immediacy, micro- versus macrohistorical trends, and contingency versus the constraints of nature. While historians are inclined to accept "the otherness of the past," there is also considerable emphasis on collective memory (especially in relation to identity). This fosters a sense of historical immediacy that threatens to erase the proper divide between past and present.[18] David Lowenthal perceptively notes that at the same time that the past "grows ever more foreign" for historians, the public "cannot bear so alien a past, and strenuously domesticate it," and so "rather than a foreign country, the past becomes our sanitized own."[19] Although microhistory is much in vogue, history on a much larger scale is also robust, as is evident by the work produced by Atlantic, world, and global historians. And while many contemporary historians embrace contingency and human agency, environmental historians are providing valuable information about the impact of climate and geography on human societies. In doing so, these historians are establishing the physical parameters for human activity and choices.

These last examples suggest something else. Developments in the world may have as much impact on historical inquiry as those that occur within the academy. Keith Thomas contends that most of the "fashionable historical topics of the present time owe their vogue to essentially non-academic preoccupations." Historical studies of memory testify to the legacy of the Holocaust; enthusiasm for environmental history is no doubt partially a function of concern about global warming and scarcity of natural resources; and historical interest in empire owes much to American foreign policy.[20]

Though David Cannadine suspects that "the notion of history in crisis seems to have been around as long as people have been writing history," it is fair to say that history is a much calmer discipline than it was in the 1990s. This is not to suggest that history does not face significant challenges. Sam Wineburg's remarks in this volume certainly point to serious work that needs to be done in history education and understanding the transmission of historical memory from one generation to the next. And there is genuine concern that specialization in historical subfields breeds a lamentable fragmentation in the discipline, as well as what Cannadine calls "sub-disciplinary chauvinism, where some practitioners insistently assert the primacy of their approach to the past and show little sympathy with, or knowledge of, other approaches."[21]

The journal *Historically Speaking* was launched at a time when many believed—not without some justification—that history was still in crisis. The hope was that it would become a different type of historical publication, one that would provide a congenial and accessible venue for scholars and educators from across the subdisciplinary and methodological spectra to enter into conversation with each other. It would not avoid controversial subjects; neither would it be embarrassed to publish responsible arguments that run against the grain. Intellectual exchange cannot occur unless opposing viewpoints have a place at the table. *Historically Speaking* has played a modest role in moving the discipline from crisis mode to more constructive dialogue. Only then can we address concerns such as those voiced by Wineburg and Cannadine. From its inception *Historically Speaking* has paid special attention to the state of historical thinking. The essays and interviews in this volume, drawn from the pages of *Historically Speaking* from 2002 to 2006, attest to this interest and demonstrate the value of encouraging historians to be in conversation.

NOTES

1. Keith Thomas, "New Ways Revisited: How History's Borders Have Expanded in the Past Forty Years," *Times Literary Supplement,* October 13, 2006, 4.

2. Richard J. Evans, prologue, "What Is History?—*Now,*" *What Is History Now?,* ed. David Cannadine (Houndmills, Basingstoke, U.K.: Palgrave Macmillan, 2002), 9.

3. Thomas, "New Ways Revisited," 3. See, for example, Darren Oldridge, *Strange Histories* (New York: Routledge, 2005).

4. Thomas, "New Ways Revisited," 3; Felipe Fernández-Armesto, epilogue, "What Is History *Now?*" in *What Is History Now?,* 155.

5. David Cannadine, preface, *What Is History Now?* (2002), xi.

6. John Lukacs, "Popular and Professional History," *Historically Speaking* 3 (April 2002): 2–5.

7. Evans, prologue, 15. It is both curious and troubling that the public's seemingly insatiable appetite for history coexists with concerns over the status of history

(as opposed to social studies) at the secondary level, as well as the overemphasis placed on specialized and largely inaccessible scholarly monographs (as opposed to excellence in classroom teaching) in college and university promotion and tenure decisions.

8. See Alun Munslow, *Deconstructing History* (London: Routledge, 1997), 16; Keith Jenkins, *Why History? Ethics and Postmodernity* (London: Routledge, 1999), 3.

9. Alun Munslow, *The New History* (Harlow, U.K.: Pearson Longman, 2003), 4–6.

10. Keith Windschuttle, *The Killing of History: How a Discipline Is Being Murdered by Literary Critics and Social Theorists* (Paddington, Australia: Macleay, 1996).

11. See Richard J. Evans, *In Defense of History* (New York: Norton, 1999), 219–20; Marc Trachtenberg, "The Past under Siege: A Historian Ponders the State of His Profession—and What to Do about It," in *Reconstructing History: The Emergence of a New Historical Society,* ed. Elizabeth Fox-Genovese and Elisabeth Lasch-Quinn (New York: Routledge, 1999), 9–11.

12. See Eugene D. Genovese, "A New Departure," in *Reconstructing History, Reconstructing History,* 7.

13. Fernández-Armesto, epilogue, 149.

14. Thomas, "New Ways Revisited," 4.

15. Fernández-Armesto, epilogue, 149.

16. Thomas, "New Ways Revisited," 4.

17. Evans, prologue, 8–9. See also Thomas, "New Ways Revisited," 4.

18. Allan Megill, "Are We Asking Too Much of History?" *Historically Speaking* 3 (April 2002): 11.

19. David Lowenthal, "The Past of the Future: From the Foreign to the Undiscovered Country, *History Today* 56 (June 2006): 46.

20. Thomas, "New Ways Revisited," 4.

21. Cannadine, preface, xi.

PART 1

The State of Historical Inquiry

Are We Asking Too Much of History?

Allan Megill

In a much-quoted statement in the preface of his *Histories of the Latin and Germanic Nations* (1824), the young Leopold Ranke remarked that "history has been assigned the office of judging the past, of instructing the present for the benefit of future ages." Ranke demurred: *his* work, he tells his readers, "wants only to say what actually happened." Ranke was reacting against earlier views that gave history the task of being a preceptor of life (*historia magistra vitae,* as the tag had it), offering general rules by which we might guide our actions. He was surely justified in rejecting the morally and pragmatically oriented approaches to history that he found in earlier writers. First, such history could only produce distorted representations of the past. Second, the claim to offer lessons in ethics and prudence was fraudulent, for such-and-such actions in the past were judged to be exemplary but on the basis of pre-existing ethical views. The resulting history was thus an exercise in false confirmation, giving back to the present the present's own prejudices dressed up in the garb of antiquity. Third, this history misrepresented the *present* as much as it did the past. Although his political stance was radically opposed to Ranke's, Karl Marx made much the same point at the beginning of *The Eighteenth Brumaire of Louis Bonaparte,* where he notes how images taken from the past obscure people's apprehension of the world as it actually is. Had it been relevant to his argument, Marx might also have pointed out that the contrary is also true, for the search for lessons from the past obscures our apprehension of the world as it actually *was.*

From *Historically Speaking* 3 (April 2002). Parts of this essay appear in the conclusion of Allan Megill, *Historical Knowledge, Historical Error* (2007).

What might a Ranke *redivivus* say about the tasks that are assigned to history today? In Ranke's day only a few, the highest elite, could do the assigning. Today multitudes crowd the scene, both rulers and *demos,* both producers and consumers of history, clad in varied clothing and clamoring loudly. They include state legislators, intent on the right teaching of history in the schools and colleges of their fine states; federal legislators, horrified at the historical ignorance of college students and of the general public; generous donors, intent on establishing a chair for the history of this and a chair for the history of that; Americans proud of their ethnic heritage or religion, who want to make sure that its glories are properly represented and celebrated; veterans of wars, eager to see that the wars in question are both correctly interpreted and piously commemorated; and those persons bereaved by, or perhaps only touched by, all major disasters, most recently the shocking events of September 11, 2001. Beyond these persons or groups, who have an entirely explicit and active concern with history, are others whose concern is more diffuse and consumption oriented. I think here of those who "appreciate" history in the way that one might appreciate an appealing wallpaper pattern or a nicely manicured front lawn—who visit presidential houses, stop at battlefields and at historical sites of other kinds, perhaps pause in their travels to read historical markers, and in general admire oldish things. Their appreciation sometimes goes so far as to express itself in the assertion, "I have always loved history."

In short, Clio has many friends and perhaps some lovers. But love and friendship are not without their price. The fans clamoring around ask for more things than the judging and instructing that worried Ranke. The tasks that are today assigned to history seem to be of four types. First and foremost, there is assigned to history the task of *identifying*—of creating and sustaining identities of various kinds and hence of making "us" (whoever "us" is) feel good about ourselves. Crucial to this task is the related enterprise of commemorating the actions and especially the sufferings of those individuals and (especially) groups who are thus identified. Second, history is assigned the task of *evangelizing*—of strengthening our civic religion. Third, history is given the task of *entertaining* us. Finally, to history is assigned the task, where possible, of *being useful.* To be sure, it is acknowledged that history cannot be quite as useful as engineering, business administration, and animal husbandry, and it is widely held as well that some history, usually that which is distant from us in time, space, or culture, cannot be useful at all. Hence this fourth task pales before the other three.

Am I mistaken in thinking that these tasks—especially the tasks of identifying, evangelizing, and entertaining—are widely assigned to history today?

I think not. Consider the distribution network for history books, a network that, thanks to the Internet, is more visible now than in the past. Definite claims and assumptions concerning history recur in the advertising that emanates from such Web sites as www.amazon.com and www.barnesandnoble .com.

I have perused advertisements appearing in several e-mail newsletters intended by Amazon.com for history buffs (I have also looked in a more casual way at the blurbs for best-selling history books that come up when one browses the subject "history" on Amazon). I here reproduce the text of three advertisements, drawn seriatim from Amazon.com's history e-mail newsletter of May 11, 2001:

Pearl Harbor: The Day of Infamy—An Illustrated History by Dan van der Vat. President Franklin D. Roosevelt famously declared December 7, 1941 as "A day that will live in infamy," the day the Japanese attacked Pearl Harbor, pulling the U.S. into World War II. This visually stunning book, by noted historian Dan van der Vat, features groundbreaking research, over 250 images, including previously unpublished personal photos from the perspective of both Americans on the ground and Japanese in the air, as well as a moment-by-moment breakdown of the attack. There are also numerous personal accounts, memorabilia, and illustrations by Tom Freeman. A major achievement.

An Album of Memories: Personal Histories from the Greatest Generation by Tom Brokaw. As he's done in his immensely popular Greatest Generation volumes, Tom Brokaw again celebrates the trials and triumphs of the Americans who experienced the Depression and World War II. *Album of Memories* is a collection of letters written to Brokaw by those who lived during this period, and in some cases, their children. Complete with photographs and memorabilia, the overall emotional impact of these letters is intense. To read them is both a moving experience and an opportunity to experience history at its most intimate.

Disaster! The Great San Francisco Earthquake and Fire of 1906 by Dan Kurzman. Just after 5 A.M. on April 18, 1906, an earthquake measuring 8.3 on the Richter scale ripped through sleeping San Francisco, toppling buildings, exploding gas mains, and trapping thousands of citizens beneath tons of stone, broken wood, and twisted metal. Drawing on meticulously researched and eye-witness accounts, Dan Kurzman re-creates one of the most horrific events of the twentieth century. More riveting than fiction but incredibly true, *Disaster!* is unforgettable history—a masterful account of the calamitous demise and astonishing resurrection of an American city.

I do not aim to score cheap points against works that no one expects to live up to the standards of scientific history. I refer to these works only because they reveal an orientation toward history widespread in present-day American culture and perhaps also in modern culture generally. I also suspect that this orientation has made inroads into the discipline, although in a casual essay I cannot develop my points at length or justify them adequately.

The idea that history might be ethically or pragmatically useful is absent from the above examples. Nothing so distancing as an ethically normative idea makes its appearance. The advertising for *An Album of Memories* suggests that Tom Brokaw deals with "the trials and triumphs" of the "greatest generation" in order to celebrate those endeavors and to give his audience a "moving experience." Implied is that history can give us an emotional empathy with past human beings, but what seems important here is the frisson of an immediate relation. The claim that history might have a *pragmatic* utility is also absent from these examples. But very few works of history dare to make this sort of claim: they constitute a small and specialized genre, one that usually emanates from people connected more to a policy-oriented political science than to history. On the other hand, history's other contemporary functions are all proudly on display, so closely intertwined in the minds of the publicity people as to be almost indistinguishable. Most obviously, an appeal is made to American identity, particularly in *Pearl Harbor* and *An Album of Memories*. All the books evangelize, propagating what can be best described as a can-do faith, one that affirms our capacity to overcome the difficulties that life brings, even earthquakes. Along with the identifying and the evangelizing comes the promise of great entertainment—we are being offered experiences that are "visually stunning," "intense," and "riveting."

No doubt the advertisements' highlighting of entertainment value is to be expected, given that the books are all aimed at a mass audience. Obviously one cannot *directly* turn from popular history of this sort to the writing, teaching, and other related activities of professional historians. There are nonetheless convergences between the two spheres that make a reflection on these popular modes relevant to the professional enterprise of historical research and writing at the beginning of the twenty-first century. The most obvious locus of convergence is to be found in the sphere of computer applications. Such applications claim to offer something that is also very evident in the advertising copy. They offer immediacy—or at least a simulacrum of immediacy. Some of the more recent historical documentaries to be seen on television make a similar promise (they differ from an older generation of documentaries, such as Thames Television's 1973–74 series on World War II,

The World at War, where the presentation is much more depersonalized and "objective"). A few mornings ago my dental hygienist, noting that she "loved history," mentioned the latest production by Ken Burns. New technology, particularly Microsoft's PowerPoint, makes it possible for the average historian to be Ken Burns–like in classroom lectures. Soon, job candidates who neglect to prepare lectures using PowerPoint will be putting themselves out of the running for jobs at colleges where the central emphasis is on teaching. A lecture on sixteenth-century Augsburg, for example, will be so much more appealing to a lower-level undergraduate audience when the lecturer can scan in lots of visuals and project them as needed.

If I *have* to attend a lecture for lower-level undergraduates on a subject not expected to appeal to them, I would rather it include visuals than not.[1] My concern is not to reject the technology but to draw attention to certain dangers inherent in it. Consider again the identity-oriented attitude toward history (with its heavy concern for commemoration and memorialization), the assumption that a central task of history is to affirm and strengthen our ideals and the insistence that history should be entertaining. Consider, further, the heavy emphasis that is given—at least in many colleges and universities—to the histories of those entities that are thought to be close to us (our own country, even our own region). Consider also the impact on thinking of certain aspects of the new technologies. (For example, I was recently struck by a presentation given by a "digital historian," who took it as a given, without adducing any argument, that such-and-such a debatable historical claim was true and who then focused almost entirely on how this truth could be most strikingly presented, in a Web-based form, to the public.) And consider the ideological and interest- or identity-group pressures that are exerted on history. To be sure, none of these orientations and tendencies should be rejected entirely. History is, after all, an impure science. Yet at the same time they need to be resisted.

The core of the difficulty lies in the claim to historical immediacy. The claim can be found almost everywhere. The advertising cited above uniformly suggests that consumers of history will be brought into direct contact with the action. Note how the advertisements focus on personal experience. We are told that "one of the most horrific events of the twentieth century"—the San Francisco earthquake of 1906—will be "re-created" by the author. We are told that reading letters written to a news anchor by "Americans who experienced the Depression and World War II" is "both a moving experience and an opportunity to experience history at its most intimate." The photos in *Pearl Harbor,* taken "from the perspective of both Americans on the ground and

Japanese in the air," likewise seem to promise a virtual reliving of the attack. The book *Pearl Harbor* was issued at about the time that a "major motion picture" focused on Pearl Harbor came out. The "tie-in" was intended. *Pearl Harbor* the movie was not a historical documentary but a lame love story. Still, it attempted to convey, in its sequence showing the attack on Pearl Harbor, the impression of "you are there." Consider another entertainment, the 1997 movie *Titanic*—likewise not a historical documentary but a brilliantly realized tragic romance. The producers of *Titanic* made a self-conscious appeal to historical authenticity, for they went to enormous lengths to duplicate the look of the original ship and its furnishings. Here historical immediacy turns into an aesthesis of history, an attempt to get viewers as close as possible to the sight and sound of historical reality itself. The producers were on to something—they rightly intuited that, for a vast audience, history, if it does not mean "dead and gone, irrelevant," means the immediate representation of objects from the past.[2]

But the promise of immediacy is not to be found *only* in popular history books or in the history put together by video documentarians or in the historical aspect of popular entertainments. It is also to be found in the work of professional historians and of others connected with them (most often, museum professionals). This is hardly surprising. After all, *identifying* history is overwhelmingly concerned with what it takes to be "our" identity; *evangelizing* history with what it takes to be "our" faith. Hence the attempts that curators make at Colonial Williamsburg, Plimoth Plantation, and other similar sites to reproduce the "look" and "feel" of life in an earlier time. One sees the same impulse in some digital "archives," those driven by a concern for making "everything" that exists concerning a given past time and place available in a single set of Web pages, with the aim of enabling the browsing public to enter into the life of a past community or the flux of a set of past events. Let us leave aside the problems that exist on the evidentiary level—above all, the quaint assumption that all evidence relevant to explaining X in some given time and place is localized within that time and place (whereas the universe of *possibly* relevant evidence is in fact unbounded, its *actual* boundaries only determinable through continuing argument). The deeper problem is the making of a promise that can never be fulfilled. Consider also the growing number of projects that combine, virtually in a single entity, features of the archive, museum, and memorial. No doubt there is a kind of catharsis and reflectiveness that can be achieved by standing in the place of (even taking the number of) a Holocaust victim, and there is perhaps also the confirming of an identity. But again the assumption of immediate identification is left epistemologically unjustified, while, on the interpretive level, the stakes of the identification are kept implicit, hence unargued, hence uncontroverted, hence undefended in any full sense of the term. Consider, finally, a certain kind of historical biography, the kind that aims at recreating what we might call "the inner Mr. X" (for "Mr. X" substitute any historical figure). Never mind whether a sense of *Innerlichkeit* is applicable to Mr. X in quite the way that it is applicable to "us," "now."[3]

The question with which I began was: Are we asking too much of history? At first glance it might seem that we are. In wishing to "say what actually happened," Ranke was not at all concerned with unveiling events as they immediately felt to historical actors and sufferers. Rather, as he makes perfectly clear in his 1824 preface, his aim was to give an accurate account of "the beginning of modern history." To this project anything like the present-day identity historians' concern for giving readers an immediate "feel" of the past was utterly irrelevant, besides being inconceivable for a man situated as Ranke was. But it seems to me more accurate to say that present-day identity historians and their friends are asking *too little* of history. For what is missing in the pursuit of the identifying, evangelizing, entertaining, and utility functions of history is precisely the sense of any fundamental break between present and past. In a certain sense the history that is close to us is a dangerous history, precisely because it *is* close. One cannot deny that history is tied up with present identities, but to make those identities fundamental seems to me a fundamental mistake. Rather than focusing on how history might create and sustain identity, which in most circumstances can look after itself, and which in some circumstances, such as those of religious or ethnic conflict, is a positive danger, historians ought to attend more fully to the critical function of history. I do not mean that historians ought to turn themselves into practitioners of critical theory. What I mean is that they ought to attend more fully to the critical dimension of the historical discipline *itself.* Rather than seeking to bolster present identity by linkage to the past, historians in their critical function ought to highlight what divides past from present. Here it ought to be a matter not of showing continuity between past and present but rather of showing how the past provides a reservoir of alternative possibilities, of paths not taken, of difference. There is within all historical writing the danger of a retrospective illusion: because the past followed a particular path, we are inclined to think that it *had* to follow that path. In a globalized society, wherein (at least at some levels) homogenization takes place, it is important to articulate true representations that make vivid other ways of understanding the world than the ways that are our own.[4]

NOTES

1. Of course, there are undergraduates and then there are undergraduates: perhaps the proper description for the audience should be "people assumed to be not very interested in history." Those of us who teach at institutions filled with intellectually curious and lively lower-level students can only regard with awe the efforts of those who have to try to *generate* such curiosity and engagement.

2. Somewhat ironically, the attempted closeness actually underscored the historical *in*authenticity of *Titanic,* because the characters of the drama—their dress, physiques, bearing, voices, language, class relations, desires, sexual behavior, and aspirations—all had to be calculated according to what a present-day audience would find understandable, empathetic, and interesting. The *characters* thus clashed quite dramatically with the *furnishings.*

3. Pity the historical biographer nowadays who discovers that his subject has no *Innerlichkeit* whatsoever. This may in part explain the disastrous fictionalized biography of Ronald Reagan by Edmund Morris, *Dutch: A Memoir of Ronald Reagan* (New York: Random, 1999). In any case, where identity is uppermost, evidence tends to be cast aside as irrelevant—a fact that might also help explain the lies that another historian and biographer, Joseph Ellis, told about his personal history.

4. The theoretical perspective that I articulate here is in part suggested in, and exemplified by Michel de Certeau, *The Writing of History,* trans. Tom Conley (New York: Columbia University Press, 1988).

What Is History Now?

An Interview with David Cannadine

What does it mean to study history? In his 1961 Trevelyan Lectures at Cambridge University, E. H. Carr asked this question, and his answer, *What Is History?* is still widely read and debated today. David Cannadine has edited a collection of essays, *What Is History Now?* (2002), presented at a 2001 conference at London's Institute of Historical Research and dedicated to reviewing the state of the discipline forty years after Carr's lectures.

Given the enduring importance of Carr's question and the new light being cast on it, Donald A. Yerxa interviewed Cannadine for *Historically Speaking.*

DONALD A. YERXA: *What Is History Now?* is the product of a two-day symposium hosted in November 2001 by the Institute of Historical Research in London. What was the purpose of this gathering?

DAVID CANNADINE: The Institute of Historical Research is a place where we pride ourselves on bringing together historians of different backgrounds and viewpoints to discuss a variety of issues at meetings and conferences. And we thought that the fortieth anniversary of the publication of E. H. Carr's *What Is History?* would be a good time both to reevaluate the book and to think about how and where history has moved on in the intervening period. So we had a two-day symposium with more than two hundred people here, and a hugely interesting time was had, after which we have been able to produce this book.

From *Historically Speaking* 4 (February 2003)

YERXA: Why have historians considered Carr's *What Is History?* a classic treatment of historical method and inquiry?

CANNADINE: It is interesting to think that Carr's book, written originally as the Trevelyan Lectures at Cambridge University, came out in the early 1960s as an attempt to provide a synoptic account of what history appeared to be about at that time. He set out a rather panoramic account of what he thought history was, which in many ways set the agenda for how history actually did develop in the 1960s and 1970s. *What Is History?* was enormously important at that time because it did appear to tell people what historians were doing or should be doing. And since then, of course, as history has moved on, it has become something of a period-piece classic. Having been in a sense a manifesto for the 1960s and 1970s, it has now become a retrospective monument to the 1960s and 1970s—to the way that people did history then but, in some senses, don't do history now.

YERXA: The obvious question then is what are some of the more significant ways that historical inquiry has been altered in the four decades since Carr's work first appeared?

CANNADINE: Carr emphasized the primacy of long-term economic and social forces, which he thought drove the historical process forward. He thought that extra-European history was an important subject that deserved far more attention that it was receiving at the time. He thought that history should be interdisciplinary, and we should learn from sociology. He thought history was all about explanation, about causes, about why things change. And he thought that, on the whole, individuals didn't matter very much. So, in a nutshell, Carr believed that history ought to be written in the 1960s with an emphasis on long-term economic and social forces, with minimal stress on the importance of the individual, with recognition of the world as a whole rather than just Britain, and with focus on causation and explanation, rather than narrative or biography. And a lot of people did write history in the 1960s and on into the early 1970s in the manner Carr suggested. If one thinks of books like Lawrence Stone's *Crisis of the Aristocracy* or E. P. Thompson's *Making of the English Working Class,* these were very much written in that sort of way. They were about change, they were about economic and social development, and they were about collective modes of behavior rather than about specific individuals. But I think over the last fifteen to twenty years the priorities of historians have, to some degree, shifted: sociology and economics are much less important interdisciplinary influences than they were two generations ago. Anthropology is a much more powerful influence now. We are much less sure about long-term economic and social forces determining outcomes than once we were. Randomness and the quirks of individual personality and decisions matter a lot. All of which means that many historians no longer believe the search for causes, for explanations, is worth undertaking; rather, they think we ought to come to terms with meaning and understanding—that is, to try to imagine ourselves into earlier worlds where people saw things quite differently from the way we see them now. Meaning and understanding—often built around individual episodes or stories or lives —have now taken the center stage in a way that long-term economic and social change did for Carr.

YERXA: Carr tended to view history as more of a scientific than a literary endeavor. Yet these days we are witnessing—in the United States at least—an emphasis on the themes of contingency, human agency, and narrative tension. Do you see this as a positive development, or have we gone too far in this direction, perhaps?

CANNADINE: I am fairly agnostic about phases and fashions in history writing; they come and go. That's part of the fun of the subject. History possesses an amazing capacity to renew itself; historians invent new areas of inquiry, new approaches to the past, and new methodologies and modes of exposition. Different approaches to historical inquiry have come and gone during the twentieth century, as one fashion follows another. Sooner or later each peaks and declines as something else takes over. But that's how history gets moved forward; new ideas, new approaches come in. So the whole process of understanding the rich complexity of the historical enterprise becomes more sophisticated and more varied, richer and more nuanced. On the whole, that is a good thing.

YERXA: On both sides of the Atlantic, there was a fair amount of concern registered during the 1990s about a crisis in the historical profession. Many historians wrote about the potentially debilitating effects of fragmentation and overspecialization, the trivialization of historical inquiry resulting from an emphasis on "the irrational, the eccentric and the bizarre," and the threat posed by those who proclaimed the seeming impossibility of historical knowledge. Yet you and your contributors certainly do not portray a profession in crisis. What has changed?

CANNADINE: The notion of history in crisis seems to have been around as long as people have been writing history. After all, history was thought to be in crisis in the 1900s, on the one side, because some people thought it was too literary and, on the other side, because some people thought it was too scientific. History was thought to be in crisis in the 1960s because some people thought it was too sociological and quantitative, and others thought it wasn't sociological and quantitative enough. This is part of the process whereby new subjects or new subspecializations are taken on board and integrated. And it is entirely predictable to have some people say, "This is wonderful; this is new; it is the only way to go; we must do it." And others will say, "This is all dreadful and deplorable; it will erode a long tradition of a different sort of scholarship; and therefore history is in crisis." I think we've just had the latest version of that in the 1990s with postmodernism and all the things connected with that. Advocates claimed that it opened a whole new range of possibilities in terms of who could be involved, the subjects dealt with, and so on. Other people saw it as a threat to the very nature of history because they claimed it denied that we can know the truth about anything. And it seems to me that talk in the 1990s of history in crisis was just another one of these battles that are fought out every generation over what history is about.

YERXA: You mention that "history as practiced during the first decade of the twenty-first century is going through an exceptionally vigorous, lively, and innovative period." Where do you see the greatest cause for hope and celebration?

CANNADINE: There is broad public interest in history—an appetite for history—both within the academy and outside the academy, on television, in museums, in local history societies, and so on, which is more vigorous than it has ever been before. I think in all those ways, the climate for history, the curiosity about the past, the appetite to know and learn more has never been stronger. Fortunately there are more historians on both sides of the Atlantic writing the sort of imaginative history books that help quench that appetite, if one quenches appetites, which I feel one probably doesn't. People like Niall Ferguson, Linda Colley, or Felipe Fernández-Armesto are writing books on large themes that enthrall the public as well as impress academic colleagues. And that, it seems to me, is a very hopeful sign. Now others might view all this differently: there's too much going on; history is losing its coherence; it's all over the place; nobody knows what we are doing anymore. After all, one person's vigorous history is another's chaotic history. Clearly, I'm on the side of those who think that it is vigorous.

YERXA: In the late 1990s, you suggested that there was tension between an academic culture of productivity at odds with a culture of creativity and, presumably, quality. Is that still the case?

CANNADINE: There is certainly reason for concern in Britain. I maintain that in many ways history is very buoyant as a subject, but British academic historians teaching in British universities are not buoyant as a professional group. And that is because they are part of a larger professional group—British academics employed in British universities—who are working in an environment that is underfunded, underesteemed, overregulated, and extremely regimented. That is not an ideal environment for very creative work. To be sure, a few historians manage to transcend the limits and inadequacies of that environment and still produce great books, but they do that despite their professional environment, not because of it.

YERXA: There has been considerable discussion in recent years about the question of popular versus academic history. In your volume, Felipe Fernández-Armesto describes what he sees as a separation of the historical profession from the public as something of a crisis. What is your assessment of the current state of popular history?

CANNADINE: This is another one of these questions that has been around as long as historians have been writing. Recall the debate in the 1900s as to whether history was an art or a science. If history was indeed a science, then it should stay within the ivory tower. But if history was an art, it should reach a broader public. So this argument has been going for at least one hundred years, and it will doubtless continue. It has been reinforced and reignited, I suppose, by the huge appeal of several very famous historians on the television, which makes that apparent polarity between academic and popular history seem even more marked. My own opinion is that it is a false dichotomy. An increasing number of academic historians do accept that they ought be writing not just for each other but for a broader public audience and that history is part of national culture. If one of the ways of doing that is appearing on television in addition to writing books, then so be it; that is one of the mediums that we live with now. After all, if one thinks of the most successful television historians—Simon Schama or David Starkey, or indeed Felipe Fernández-Armesto himself—those are all people with impeccable academic credentials and with academic jobs. So I think it is rather misleading to draw an adversarial picture of academics who are somehow doing serious research versus popularizers on the television. Back in the 1950s or 1960s, in the days of A. J. P. Taylor or Kenneth Clark, there was a huge appetite for charismatic, scholarly performers talking about history. And that's still true today; the only thing that has changed is that there are more of them now—there are more television programs now—than there were then. In fact we had a conference at the Institute of Historical Research in December 2002 on history in the media, and we got to discuss a whole set of these issues.

YERXA: What do you see as the greatest challenges to historical inquiry?

CANNADINE: In many ways the greatest challenges for historical inquiry remain what they always were: whether it is possible for historians, either in the universities or outside, to live in environments that do not tolerate freedom of research, freedom of thought, and freedom of expression. If one looks at the twentieth century, it is important to remember that while in most parts of the West, history has grown and advanced and become an essential part of national life, in many nations elsewhere in the world, history has been one of the great casualties of war, tyranny, barbarism, and revolution. In many nations the presumption that there is a trustworthy historical account of life in an earlier time is something that cannot be taken for granted. We normally do tend to take that for granted in the West. But elsewhere, for much of the twentieth century, that could not have been taken for granted. So it seems to me that the most important danger to history is the danger that it actually cannot be practiced as a serious profession and that it cannot be part of national culture. There are still many repressive regimes that do not want to hear the truth about the past any more than they want to hear the truth about the present. Historians are people of integrity and passion, who stand for truth and for freedom, but there are still far too many places in the world today where both of those things are regarded as anathema.

On the Current State of History

An Interview with Richard J. Evans

R ichard J. Evans is professor of modern history at Cambridge University. A specialist in German social and cultural history, Evans is also widely known for his multivolume history of the Third Reich and his historiographical writing, especially *In Defense of History* (1997; first published in the United States in 1999). Evans also has written a new introduction to E. H. Carr's *What Is History?* and a new afterword to G. R. Elton's *Practice of History*. The following interview was conducted on March 21, 2003.

DONALD A. YERXA: Why did you feel the need to defend history in the 1990s?

RICHARD J. EVANS: *In Defense of History* came about because I was asked to teach a lecture course on historical epistemology at Birkbeck College in London, where I was professor of history at the time, before I moved to Cambridge. As I read in preparation for the course, I discovered that the literature on questions such as "What is history?" and "How do we find out about the past?" was either very out of date (Carr and Elton, for example) or written in a spirit of extreme skepticism by postmodernist theorists (people like Keith Jenkins and Frank Ankersmit). Clearly, there was room for an up-to-date statement about historical knowledge that argued for its possibility while taking on board the criticisms of the postmodernists and trying to deal with them openly, rather than simply ignoring them. As I read more, particularly in the journals, I found that there was a good deal of debate among historians about postmodernist and poststructuralist skepticism and hyperrelativism. There were angry and dire wailings about this, without any real attempt to come to

From *Historically Speaking* 4 (June 2003)

grips with it. So I developed my lectures, and as I shared them with some colleagues, they encouraged me to expand them into a book.

YERXA: Was history in a state of crisis in the mid- to late 1990s?

EVANS: There was a widespread feeling of an epistemological crisis. Of course, a lot of historians never even realized there were these postmodernists out there, so the sense of crisis was not universal in the historical profession. But those who paid attention to these things realized that there was a serious theoretical attack under way on the nature and possibility of historical knowledge. And that did engender a sense of crisis.

YERXA: Has the sense of crisis dissipated?

EVANS: Interestingly, I think it has to a large extent. As I said in *In Defense of History*, there is a tendency for new methodological and theoretical approaches to begin by proclaiming their universal validity and their power to revolutionize the whole of historical study. Then within a short space of time, they tend to become subspecialties, with their own journals and societies where their adherents talk mainly to one another. And that is exactly what has happened to the extreme relativists among the postmodernists. Their critique has not left the practice of history unchanged, though the extreme skepticism that they voiced about historical knowledge has now subsided into a rather marginal phenomenon. After all, the only possible reaction from historians who actually did accept these notions was to stop writing history, and more history is being written today than ever before.

YERXA: What has been the legacy of these methodological debates?

EVANS: There have been negative and positive legacies. One noteworthy effect has been to direct attention to culture and language as ways of explaining and understanding history. And that has brought us away from the dominant socioeconomical model of the 1970s and 1980s, which held that society and the economy were the driving forces in history. At that time, ideas took second rank in the explanatory models of many historians. Historians now take ideas, language, and culture much more seriously, and I think that is a good thing. On the other hand, some historians have started to neglect social and economic factors and to advance a crude cultural or even linguistic determinism that is just as one-sided as the old economic determinism.

Another effect has been that we historians have become more self-conscious in our practice. In a negative sense, that can mean that historical writing becomes self-indulgent, simply the expression of personal views, quirks, and opinions. It can become a very egotistical, narcissistic exercise. On the positive side, it has caused us to become more honest about our own writing and research. This has contributed to an interesting phenomenon in the U.K.: a tremendous boom in popular history. You can see this especially on television. A British television producer recently said, "History is the new gardening," meaning that gardening programs are giving way to history programs on the TV channels. And I think that is partly because we now have presenters like Simon Schama, David Starkey, and Niall Ferguson, who give what's obviously a personal view of the past but on the basis of mostly authoritative knowledge. This is in great contrast to the way history was presented in the media fifteen or twenty years ago when you had the pictures accompanied by an impersonal, objective-sounding voice-over. Academic historians have been enabled by acceptance of the subjectivity in their own work to take part in popular history and the dissemination of historical interpretations and research, and that is a good thing.

YERXA: What gives you the greatest cause for hope as you assess the current state of historical inquiry?

EVANS: The greatest cause for hope is that professional historians are writing in a way that is much more accessible than it used to be in the 1970s and 1980s when, for all its many virtues, the social-science model of history did not have great readability or popular appeal. Historians are getting their message across to a much wider readership than they used to. And academic historians are not leaving the field to amateur historians and journalists as used to be the case. History is more diverse than it has ever been, and that's also a very positive development. There are now many different kinds of history; everything is grist for the historian's mill, and that, too, is very good.

YERXA: And what concerns you the most about the current state of history?

EVANS: There are at least two developments that give cause for concern. One is the state of history instruction in the schools, at least in the U.K. We have a national curriculum here that lays down what subjects are to be taught, and history has been squeezed by other subjects deemed by the government to be more important. The possibility of concentrating on history and to combine that with learning a foreign language seems, for example, to be now almost impossible. Consequently, there are virtually no history students, no young historians coming into the profession in this country who speak any foreign languages at all. Thus none of my Ph.D. students who are working on subjects in German and European continental history is British: they are German, Swiss, Canadian, American, and so on. That is a pity. The great tradition of British historians who work on France, Germany, Russia, and other countries is coming to an end. Those subjects will continue to be taught in British universities, but they will be taught more and more by people from those countries. Interestingly these people will have taken all their degrees in

British universities, so their intellectual formation at least is partly British, and that perhaps is something of a compensating factor.

Also in the schools here there is an overwhelming concentration on the twentieth century in history teaching, and there is an appalling ignorance and lack of teaching on any period before 1914. Large swaths of history are simply going untaught, and that, too, is a great pity. So the state of history in the schools gives me great cause for concern.

The other thing that I find worrying is connected with one of the more questionable side effects of the postmodernist emphasis on subjectivity, and that is what one might call the moralization and legalization of history. By this I mean that since the early 1990s, historical studies have become more and more concerned with using moral and legal categories instead of understanding and explanation, based on value-neutral explanatory models and theories from the social sciences. And that is because many historians now deem neutrality to be morally undesirable. In a number of areas, the main concern of young historians seems to be to reach moral judgments—regarding the Crusades, slavery in the American South, Nazi Germany, or whatever it might be. There are historians working almost exclusively with concepts such as perpetrators, bystanders, victims, and so on, which don't help us understand the historical process in any way. They simply assign praise and blame.

YERXA: What do you make of the emphasis on identity and memory?

EVANS: Identity can be a very interesting way of approaching history. One of history's main functions can be to illustrate the possibilities of human thought and behavior, what it means to be human, what forms human identity can take. While there are quite a few unsatisfactory books about identity (and the concept as such is a very slippery one), still I think it is a very interesting and important phenomenon.

On memory, it is true that there is a lot of historical work now on what some call public memory or the public commemoration of the past, and memory is an important subject for historical study. But historians need to maintain a clear distinction between history and memory. I would get worried if the study of memory became a substitute for the study of the past, and I do get a sense that in some areas there is almost more writing about how people remember the past than there is writing about the past itself. That is not generally true, of course, but in the area of Nazi Germany, for instance, there is a rapidly expanding literature on how post-1945 Europe has dealt with pre-1945 Europe. A lot of it is very good and very interesting, but I think we must study what happened before 1945 as well.

YERXA: What do you see as the central task of the historian?

EVANS: The historian's central task is to understand and to explain the past. Doing so requires certain other things; it implies, for instance, that you also have to establish accurate knowledge about the past. I also think historians have to make an attempt to recreate a sense of what it was like living in the past and what people were like in the past. History is not simply an abstract cerebral enterprise; it has a creative, imaginative side to it as well. But understanding and explanation are the key things that make history different from chronicle.

Collective Memory, History Education, and Historical Consciousness

Peter Seixas

Historians have shown considerable interest in both the study of collective memory and of history education. The former examines how ordinary people understand and use the past; the latter how students learn about the past. At first glance there should be considerable overlap and interplay between the two. But, there has been relatively little.

The study of collective memory has exploded in the past decade and a half. "Memory," as Nancy Wood notes, "is decidedly in fashion."[1] Drawing from notions rooted in the work of French sociologist Maurice Halbwachs, scholars have examined the structures that enable societies to hand down beliefs about the past from one generation to the next, the purposes for which those beliefs are mobilized, their nature and shape, and the ways they change over time.[2] While one may find an underlying nostalgia (as in Pierre Nora) or a critique of nostalgia (as in Kerwin Klein and Gabrielle Spiegel), one can study collective memory without an explicit normative stance. The goal is to understand how institutions of memory worked in the various historical circumstances in which they were constructed and maintained.

The study of history education has also experienced dramatic growth in recent years. It, too, is very much concerned with the question of how people —specifically, students and teachers—think about the past.[3] Yet there is a fundamental difference in scholarly orientation between the study of collective memory and of history education: normative policy questions are always close to the surface in the latter. What should people know? How can we improve history education? What constitutes improvement? Answers to these

From *Historically Speaking* 7 (November/December 2005)

value-laden questions form a considerable portion of the literature on history education. The normative dimension is inescapable.

It seems limited, to put it politely, for scholars to offer answers to the normative questions of history education without considering the literature on collective memory. Similarly it is narrow for those who devote their scholarly lives to the study of collective memory to ignore how the past is currently taught and transmitted to the next generation. The best responses to policy questions should take into account the many ways of understanding the past, as well as the dynamics of inertia and change that collective memory studies explore. To do so, however, requires a conceptual typology of collective memory in order to provide guidance for contemporary history education with its normative demands.

Along with a number of other scholars, I believe that the notion of historical consciousness can serve as the conceptual link between these two fields of study. But there are problems, not the least of which is ambiguity in the usage of the term. Some scholars' references to historical consciousness appear to be synonymous with collective memory. For example, in an influential essay written before the recent outpouring of collective memory scholarship, Herbert Gutman used historical consciousness to refer to how Americans think about the past.[4] An important contrasting usage comes from Hans-Georg Gadamer, who considered the appearance of historical consciousness "likely the most important revolution among those we have undergone since the beginning of the modern epoch."[5] For Gadamer, historical consciousness is a specific cultural development located in the modern era. Its achievement is "the full awareness of the historicity of everything present and the relativity of all opinions" and thus the breaking of tradition's hold. "Modern consciousness—precisely as historical consciousness—takes a reflexive position concerning all that is handed down by tradition. Historical consciousness no longer listens sanctimoniously to the voice that reaches out from the past but, in reflection on it, replaces it within the context where it took root in order see the significance and relative value proper to it."[6]

Historical consciousness here becomes a specific form of memory characterized by modernity and informed by the tools developed by professional historical scholarship (such as, a critical stance toward sources and an appreciation for the foreignness of the past). From the standpoint of history education, these tools stand as a legitimate and virtually uncontested goal. But this definition of historical consciousness, when it is used to frame intercultural comparison, suggests that only certain groups *achieve* it and only then as a result of development, intercultural contact, or educational uplift. This approach has such a Eurocentric odor that many find it unacceptable: the West *has* historical consciousness, and the rest do without until they embrace modern, Western modes of understanding.

Using historical consciousness as a bridge between the study of collective memory and history education highlights a basic conundrum at the interface between these two fields. Valorizing particular types of historical consciousness is both unavoidable—most pressingly so for those concerned with history education—and fraught with difficulty. At the Centre for the Study of Historical Consciousness at the University of British Columbia, we have had an ongoing conversation about these issues. An edited collection of papers from our opening symposium, *Theorizing Historical Consciousness,* provides a glimpse of how we might sort these matters out sufficiently to enable us to chart the future study of how people understand the past. Space does not permit me to summarize each contribution, so I must focus on only a few.[7]

Jörn Rüsen has thoroughly explored the concept of historical consciousness and has developed a four-part typology of different stances toward the past as a means of moral orientation in the present. To summarize Rüsen in highly abbreviated form:

Historical consciousness can support the continuity of fixed and unchanging moral obligations, without acknowledging any significant change over time (the traditional type).

It can draw on particular events and people from the past as a source of cultural universals that apply across temporal change, as in the celebratory history of heroes to inspire strong character in the present (the exemplary type).

It can turn toward the past in order to break from it, as in feminist history that helps to undo the past's oppressive gender relations (the critical type).

It can acknowledge the ongoing legacy of the past at the same time that it comprehends radically changed present circumstances (the genetic type).

Rüsen proposes this typology as a hierarchy in terms of cognitive and moral complexity. Thus it acts as a lens through which to examine both individual and sociocultural development. Clearly there are risks and rewards from the theoretical linkage of individual and sociocultural development. Rüsen is fully aware of the danger of an overly linear, one-dimensional model of progress that takes the cultural tools of modern Europe as the goal for all cultures. There is also a risk in fashioning psychological models of development a priori from sociocultural models, without the empirical work necessary to substantiate the types as they are defined. Rüsen himself points out the difficulty in locating any particular individual along this continuum. Indeed, he writes, "Elements of all four types are operatively intermixed in the procedure which gives practical life a historical orientation in time."

Rüsen's scheme leaves largely undefined the relationship between disciplinary practices and various types of historical consciousness. His types are defined in terms of the experience of time, perceptions of historical significance, and moral judgments, values, and reasoning. Rüsen does little to relate these orientations explicitly to other fundamentally defining practices of historians, such as the critical reading of textual evidence. Further work is needed to define the relationships between disciplinary history and "advancement" in historical consciousness, as framed by Rüsen. As uncomfortable as such whiggish phraseology may be to some, a notion of advancement must undergird normative prescriptions for history education that answers the question: What should we cultivate in the way of historical consciousness in the next generation? Rüsen takes us far beyond the vacuous answer: "Teach more history."

When we take up the problem of history education directly, the question again emerges: What is needed in this culture at this time in the way of understandings of the past? Over the past decade and a half, scholars in history education have emphasized the importance of studying students' ideas as they come into the classroom. This focus is not merely on what factual data young people have at their disposal but also on the shapes of their narratives, the sense they make of them, and the tools they have (or fail to have) for assessing their truth and significance. In this sense the new history education studies share something important with collective memory studies: they both examine how people construct and use history. But unlike scholars in memory studies, history-education specialists struggle with normative notions of development.

Using the case study of Quebec history, Jocelyn Lètourneau and Sabrina Moisan explore the intersection of collective memory, history education, and disciplinary history. They point to the problem of teachers who are not equipped to offer interpretive schemes that challenge conventional, easily communicated views of Quebec's past. In the face of an entrenched narrative resistant to new historiography, Lètourneau and Moisan do not recommend imposing a new narrative but suggest instead that students be taught historical methodology to enable them to compare conflicting accounts and to construct complex narratives that take the world's "ambivalences and paradoxes, ambiguities and dissonances into account." A historical consciousness incorporating these qualities is not inconsistent with Rüsen's genetic type.

British history education research also has a strong and explicit notion of development. In contrast to Rüsen, the British have been less interested in the meaning of young people's narratives for practical life and more interested in second-order concepts like cause, explanation, and accounts that relate students' historical thinking to that in the discipline. Second-order concepts, Peter Lee explains, are not what history is about but what shape people's abilities to do history. The influential British notion of "progression" measures students' advancement toward the practices of academic historians, achieved through a combination of cognitive maturation and purposeful teaching. Lee defends this approach by arguing that disciplinary tools allow students to surmount epistemological and methodological dead ends. He has advanced his own hierarchical scheme of development based on close analysis of students' talk and writing on historical problems.

To what extent is the British approach championed by Lee compatible with Rüsen's scheme? What is the relationship between advancement in Rüsen's types and the critical practices of historians? Christian Laville, a long-time proponent of history education in the service of critical, participatory citizenship, fears that the notion of historical consciousness is essentially a version of nineteenth-century indoctrination on behalf of the nation, updated to meet the needs of twenty-first-century European consciousness. If this is indeed the case, then history curricula focused on building historical consciousness will not pay particular attention to history's disciplinary tools and practices. Drawing on Rüsen's work, Lee, however, connects mastering the discipline of history with the advancement of historical consciousness.

Roger Simon and his colleagues come to this conversation from a different starting point that, while pedagogical in nature, has clear commitments neither to disciplinary history nor to a particular version of collective memory. They are searching for new forms of remembrance, with questions about what we in the present owe to people in the past as we encounter evidence of profound victimization under oppressive regimes. Unlike Rüsen and Lee, Simon has not articulated any hierarchical scheme, but he does advance a normative notion of attentiveness to suffering and injustice. One might posit, however, a scale of responses ranging from indifference, through emotional reaction to suffering, to a fundamental reorientation of a reader's commitments and social relations in the present. Such an approach shares some commonality, at least in form, with Rüsen's definition of historical consciousness.

By setting broad questions of policy in history education against a backdrop of the study of collective memory and disciplinary history, as the notion of historical consciousness demands, researchers stand to gain much. Heretofore, the role of historians in history education has been to develop "governing narratives" that serve as standards for teaching. Laville, Lètourneau and Moisan, Lee, Rüsen, and Simon all move beyond this with a much more active role for students of history. Laville, Lètourneau and Moisan, and Lee embrace pedagogical visions of students able to use critical, disciplinary tools of historians in order to engage actively in constructing, interpreting, and adjudicating narrative interpretations of the past. In this conception historians' practices rather than their work become the standards for assessing history education. Laville in particular emphasizes the importance of critical disciplinary tools for enhancing participatory citizenship. Rüsen and Simon, for their part, understand the power of successful historical pedagogies for generating profound transformations in the orientation of students' lives.

When we place the debates about history education in the broader context of collective memory practices, we can help move the debates about teaching and learning history beyond the relatively narrow parameters within which they have often been pursued. At the same time, the normative concerns that have been in the forefront of history-education scholarship can enrich the scholarship of collective memory. The conversation captured in *Theorizing Historical Consciousness* does not resolve the thorny question of defining an "advanced" historical consciousness, but it does provide a solid basis for ongoing theoretical debate and empirical research both within national settings and in larger, comparative frames.

NOTES

1. Nancy Wood, *Vectors of Memory: Legacies of Trauma in Postwar Europe* (Oxford: Berg, 1999), 1.

2. See Kerwin Lee Klein, "On the Emergence of Memory in Historical Discourse," *Representations* 69 (2000): 127–50; James Wertsch, *Voices of Collective Remembering* (Cambridge, U.K.: Cambridge University Press, 2002); Michael Kammen, review of *Frames of Remembrance: The Dynamic of Collective Memory,* by Iwona Irwin-Zarecka, *History and Theory* 35 (1995): 245–61.

3. See Sam Wineburg, *Historical Thinking and Other Unnatural Acts: Charting the Future of Teaching the Past* (Philadelphia: Temple University Press, 2001); Peter Stearns, Peter Seixas, and Sam Wineburg, eds., *Knowing, Teaching, and Learning History: National and International Perspectives* (New York: New York University Press, 2000).

4. Herbert Gutman, "Historical Consciousness in Contemporary America," in *Power and Culture: Essays on the American Working Class,* ed. Herbert Gutman (New York: Pantheon, 1987).

5. Hans-Georg Gadamer, "The Problem of Historical Consciousness," in *Interpretive Social Science: A Second Look,* ed. Paul Rabinow and William M. Sullivan (Berkeley: University of California Press, 1987), 89.

6. Ibid., 90.

7. Contributors to *Theorizing Historical Consciousness* not discussed in this essay include Chris Lorenz, Mark Salber Phillips, Tony Taylor, John Torpey, and James Wertsch.

Historical Thinking Is Unnatural—
and Immensely Important

An Interview with Sam Wineburg

F or the past twenty years Sam Wineburg, professor of education at
Stanford University, has studied what he calls "historical habits of
mind." He believes that when it comes to thinking about history, a huge
gulf divides professional historians from their students. A passionate
advocate for the importance of history in our high school and college
classrooms, Wineburg has published widely on history education and
how it can be improved. His essays have appeared in journals such as
the *American Journal of Education,* the *Chronicle of Higher Education,*
and the *Journal of American History,* among others. His *Historical
Thinking and Other Unnatural Acts: Charting the Future of Teaching the
Past* (2001) won the 2002 Frederic W. Ness Award from the Association
of American Colleges and Universities for the book "that best illuminates
the goals and practices of a contemporary liberal education." Joseph S.
Lucas interviewed Wineburg in October 2005.

JOSEPH S. LUCAS: How do you carry out your research?

SAM WINEBURG: I come up with document sets, go into historians' offices,
and say, "Will you sit down and read these for me?" I just completed a study
where we gave two groups of historians—those who profess a religious sensibility and those who claim they're agnostic or atheists—documents about the
biblical exodus from Egypt. Then we gave the same historians documents
about the origins of the first Thanksgiving.

From *Historically Speaking* 7 (January/February 2006)

Whenever I do this kind of study, I sit down with the person and say, "Tell me, when I give you these texts, what are you going to do? How will you approach it?" Back in the early 1990s I did a study like this with a group of texts about Abraham Lincoln and his ideas on race. Before reading these, one historian said, "This topic calls to mind the latest book by McPherson and Blight's new book on memory. And the classic book by Bruce Catton." I asked, "Is there anything specifically that you'll do?" The historian—as historians tend to do—launched into a kind of small holding forth on everything he knew.

Here's where it gets interesting. The historian took the document and read the first words of the first sentence. Then he shifted his attention to the attribution and dwelled on it for a long time. He situated the document in place and time and came up with a series of questions that formed a kind of scaffold for the rest of his reading. He took a prepared mind into the body of the text. He had already identified the kind of document, the genre, the implications of the genre, the normal expectations you would bring to the genre. At the end of the task I said to this gentleman, "Sir, I notice when you read, this is what you did. And yet when I asked you what you were going to do, you didn't mention this." And in a kind of dismissive wave of the hand he said, "Well, everyone does that."

I gave the same document set to about fifteen of the students in a hundred-level lecture course this historian was teaching at the time. Not a single one of these students did what their professor had done. These findings correspond to what I discovered when I first performed this kind of study nearly twenty years ago. Historians do this kind of reading of the source 99 percent of the time. And bright undergraduates on their way to good colleges—taking AP courses, scoring well on the SAT—do this less than one-third of the time (and when they do, it's usually because they've come across a pronoun and aren't sure what it refers to). The kind of textured interrogation that comes automatically—but not naturally—to historians is a very special skill.

Historical thinking is unnatural. It goes against the grain of how we ordinarily think. We are psychologically conditioned to see unity between past and present. I have a colleague who teaches at Queen's University in Belfast. He gives his undergraduates a 1562 quote from Queen Elizabeth where she refers to the Irish as "mere Irish," at which point the Catholic kids take umbrage. But when you go to the *Oxford English Dictionary* and look at sixteenth-century references for "mere," it means "pure, unadulterated"—it's a compliment, not an insult. It is a psychological challenge to check every word, to read documents from the past and constantly ask, "Does this word mean the same thing that I think it means now?"

There is an effect in the brain called the spread of activation. When we read or hear certain things, pathways in the brain that hold that information in a localized area are highlighted or excited. We can't stop that process. That goes on automatically. But historical thinking creates—in a way that is not natural—a kind of caution. It brings to the fore certain questions that alert us to the fissure between past and present, and we begin to say, "I register the emotional reaction that I'm having to this text. But I have to stop myself. Is the past simply a convex image of the present, or have there been fundamental changes? Is there both continuity and change? I suspect that what I'm reading could mean something different from what I think it means." This is a cultivated way of approaching texts that you will not find among undergraduates. It's not what happens when we go to the movies as laypeople and see *Alexander* or watch the History Channel late at night. It's the problem of students saying, "Well, you know, uh," when they try to understand the rise of the Nazis. They don't ask themselves questions about the context. They assume a fundamental, timeless past, to use David Lowenthal's term. They mush past and present, and everything becomes the here and now. And that is something that historical thinking, done in a mature way, tries to chip away at.

LUCAS: Do you think that this way of reading and thinking is something that teachers at both the college and the secondary level try to impart to their students? Is that the key to successful history teaching?

WINEBURG: Our young people come to us from high schools where they see the learning of history as the amassing of information, and not a way of thinking and being. And so this particular way of approaching a text reflects a larger epistemology. It reflects a belief on the part of historians that the document before them is not a piece of information. It is a fragment from a human being. And one cannot engage with that fragment unless one knows to whom one is speaking. It's a fundamentally different approach. And, in that sense, we don't teach kids *explicacion de texte*. Look at the behemoths of high school textbooks—530 pages of neon-flashing gimmickry. Compare them to Charles and Mary Beard's 1935 book: a well-written, interesting text. Our kids don't know how to read carefully. Teachers, particularly in history classes, do not see close reading as one of the goals their students should strive toward.

LUCAS: Current debates over how history is taught focus on content, what's included and what's not. Are you saying that in fact it is the peculiar method of reading practiced by historians that teachers should be concentrating on?

WINEBURG: Exactly. But first of all, one qualification: I think that the discussion of content is an important discussion. We teach content. We have to have that discussion. Without the ongoing, civil argument over the kind of history that should be in the curriculum, our democracy would lose its force. In countries that don't have that discussion, you can be sure the history curriculum is without any kind of excitement or verve. I don't want to disparage the importance of having that ongoing discussion.

LUCAS: A lot of people recently have been complaining about the lack of historical knowledge on the part of both high school and college students. Was there a time when people were satisfied with the degree to which American students knew their history?

WINEBURG: Let me give you a quote: "Surely a grade of 33 out of 100 of the most basic facts of American history is not a grade of which any high school can be proud." Did this come from the 1987 National Assessment of Educational Progress report by Diane Ravitch and Chester E. Finn? Did it come from the 1976 bicentennial test that Bernard Bailyn did with the *New York Times* or the one that Allan Nevins did in 1942? No. This is a quote from a study done in Texas high schools by J. Carleton Bell and David Mc-Collum that was published in the 1918 *Journal of Educational Psychology*. It was the first large-scale factual test of American history that we have in American education. Think about who went to high school in Texas in 1915 and 1916; it must have been only 10 percent of the population, and yet they scored horribly on this test.

There is something almost natural about a group of adults wringing their hands, yearning for a time that never was. That's a chimera; it's a myth. I published an article in the *Journal of American History* in March 2004 called "Crazy for History," where I challenge the soothsayers of the historical profession: show me the money; show me the evidence. David McCullough, who continues to sell this canard, is simply wrong. He cannot adduce the documents to prove his point. It's very interesting that there are historians who claim that the basis of historical thinking is evidentiary, except when they go on the rostrums and make policy pronouncements, at which point—whether it's Sean Wilentz or McCullough—they seem to feel that they're absolved from providing the warrants for their claim.

LUCAS: Given that this is a perpetual problem, do you think that teachers in both high school and college can do a better job of getting students interested in history?

WINEBURG: Yes. In that *Journal of American History* essay, I quote a remark by Wilfred McClay from the Albert Shanker Institute's "Education for Democracy." McClay says that in times of crisis we must triage. No sentient being can comprehend our six-hundred-page textbooks. And what is at stake here is a usable narrative that can unite the disparate parts of the population and give them some basis for talking across their differences. We need to distinguish between those aspects of our history that are extraneous and those that are absolutely central to effective citizenship. My fourteen-year-old had to stop and think when I asked him if the Korean War came before or after World War II. Our young people need to understand basic issues of chronology. The aftermath of World War II created a power grab that posed the United States against the Soviet Union, which ultimately played out on the battlefields of Korea. If one doesn't understand the basic links of that narrative, how can one think about Vietnam, how can one think about the dissolution of the Soviet Union?

We cannot have the situation where we have these standards tests that ask seventeen-year-olds in Massachusetts who Ludwig von Mises was when kids don't know the Korean War—you can't have both. The mind will not countenance it. We need to make tough choices, but those tough choices have political implications. I will feel better when every single elected legislator in the state of Massachusetts sits for the factual test we give seventeen-year-olds and the results are posted in the *Boston Globe*.

But what does it mean to teach, when you presume that a foundation is in place—you are laying information and lessons on that foundation—and it turns out that it's a foundation of straw, and the very planks and concrete blocks that you envisioned to be in place are absent, and your undergraduates are totally at a loss?

Lucas: Should high school history teachers be trained differently?

Wineburg: Of course. Let's start with having them know their subject. According to data that appeared in a book I edited with Peter Stearns and Peter Seixas, 86 percent of all of the people who are teaching a subject called history in the high school or middle school curriculum have neither majored nor minored in history. We teach something in schools of education called social studies, an interesting, atavistic, kind of anachronistic, stuck-in-a-Procrustean-bed artifact of the 1930s. Until state legislatures start to pass laws saying that, just like in mathematics and just like in biology, future teachers of history should know their subject, not much is going to change.

Lucas: Do you know any really exceptional high school history teachers who are doing a great job of getting their students interested in history?

Wineburg: Absolutely. In my book there is a chapter called "Models of Wisdom in the Teaching of History," where we show and create profiles of people who are doing extraordinary things in circumstances that you would not believe—the kind of graffiti-colored, urinals-hanging-by-a-screw, urban high schools that are blights in many other respects. But you walk into the history classroom, and you've got young people of all different colors and ethnicities passionately engaged in absolutely central questions of American history. And they are learning the intellectual skills that actually might allow them to get a university degree and enter the culture of power.

Lucas: Do you think that history, as opposed to say political science or sociology or literary criticism, has a uniquely important role to play in both secondary education and the liberal arts college curriculum?

Wineburg: Without a doubt, I would say that that's my core belief. Literary criticism? I mean, we're talking about stories that aren't true. History deals with true stories. History is the training ground for the kinds of stories that we tell each other in the daily news. A knowledge of history gives us the ability to wrestle truth from the noise created by the cacophony of voices in the world. *Death in Venice* could have happened in Florence, but Kennedy's assassination didn't happen in Waco. Political science? There is obviously a lot of overlap, but history locates events in place and time and sequence and teaches us about the Kantian dimensions of human life. History teaches things that no other subject in the curriculum has even the potential to teach—not to mention the humanistic qualities, which I think are the most powerful antidote to the identity politics that riddle this country today. History teaches us that we are part of the species, that the entire history of the species is our own. And so I take membership in the species by understanding that the past is much larger than the circumstances that placed me in this particular incarnation.

Lucas: How did you get interested in history?

Wineburg: When I was nine, I received *The Illustrated History of the United States,* the American Heritage twenty-two-volume set. It was a prize possession that not only graced my bookshelf as I was growing up, but I have it today in my office. I actually refer to it quite a bit because it's a very stable narrative, and it's well done.

A second event occurred when I was ten. I found a book as we were cleaning our basement to make room for a ping-pong table. It was dog-eared, dusty, and it was entitled *Eichmann, Man of Terror.* It was the first time that I had seen black-and-white images of piles of bodies in open pits. And I sat down, and I read the book. It lit a fire. I then became a passionate reader of the first topic that I think I really plumbed in any depth, the Holocaust. I was taken aback by it, and it really brought past and present together for me.

My dad was a World War II veteran, and he never met a World War II documentary—though he died well before the History Channel—that didn't spark his interest. And he was a voracious reader of magazines. We received *Time, Life,* and *Newsweek.* My father, who was uneducated and never went to college, was very interested in topics historical. So World War II became—certainly well into high school—my frame of reference initially for viewing the past.

I had a tremendous AP U.S. history teacher in high school: Elaine Cantor, in Utica, New York. In those days we had Bailey's *American Pageant,* and often she would bring in something she had read that contradicted the main thrust of Bailey's interpretation. She would put it in front of us and say, "How do you decide?" She would ask us to write essays justifying our opinions with the evidence we had gathered.

I got my undergraduate degree from Berkeley in an interdisciplinary program devoted to religion, which was really a history of religion curriculum. I wrote an undergraduate honors thesis on a group of Jews that thrived in northern Germany prior to the First Crusade called Hasidei Ashkenaz. They were heavily influenced by the movement of monasteries from the outskirts of civilization into urban centers. And this movement, particularly in the early part of the eleventh century, resulted in books called penitentials, recipe books for the penance one would serve for particular sins. I had studied Hebrew in Israel, so I had the language skills to work with an untranslated text produced by the Hasidei Ashkenaz, *The Book of the Pious.* I argued that this was the only moment in traditional rabbinic Judaism when Jews flirted seriously with celibacy as an aim in and of itself, even though it directly contradicts the biblical injunction to be fruitful and multiply.

Lucas: How did you move from your immersion in historical research to studying historical habits of mind and how people learn and teach history?

Wineburg: I was sitting in an upper level seminar taught by Jacob Milgrom, the world's foremost expert on sacrifices in the book of Leviticus. It was a Ph.D.-level seminar—even though I was an undergraduate I got in because I had the requisite language skills. I was considering applying to Ph.D. programs in ancient history at Yale and Brandeis and was chumming around with the other Ph.D. students. One of the students in that class was just about to file her thesis. It was a 450-page dissertation on the word *prostitute, zona* in the Bible. I had an epiphany. I just couldn't see myself writing on a topic that not many people would be interested in.

I had been tutoring at an inner-city public school in Richmond, California. A position opened up for a leader of reading groups in a Chapter 1 federal program, and I took it. It seemed like a great delay tactic. I ended up delaying there for several years and realized that I was very interested in how young people read. One day I went to my supervisor and said, "I really don't understand why some kids get it and some don't." And she said, "Well, why don't you go study that in graduate school?"

I had never taken any course in psychology or education or anything on the mind—nothing. That there was even a field was a surprise to me. But I investigated it, and the rest was fate. I applied to Stanford. My application ended up on the desk of Lee Shulman, who is now the president of the Carnegie Foundation for the Advancement of Teaching. He is an educational psychologist with an undergraduate background in philosophy from the University of Chicago. He saw my lack of background in psychology as an advantage. He said that given what I'd studied already, the stuff I wanted to study in graduate school would be easy.

LUCAS: When you started graduate school, was there a body of literature on how students learn history?

WINEBURG: Absolutely none. But there was some excellent work being done on how people learn other subjects. In 1981 Andrea diSessa, an MIT physicist, published a paper in the *Journal of Cognitive Science* called "Unlearning Aristotelian Physics," which showed that MIT undergraduates, who could skillfully compute Newtonian responses to the physics problems that they were given at the end of their freshman year, nonetheless retained in a qualitative way—essentially unchanged—the beliefs that they brought to the class, which were basic Aristotelian beliefs of force and movement. This essay challenged conventional means of assessment and highlighted the intractable nature of prior beliefs and how difficult it is to unlearn them. Alan Schoenfeld, a mathematician at Hamilton College, was also doing interesting work. Both diSessa and Schoenfeld were college instructors who just became flummoxed by what they were finding among their undergraduates. They did not write in the kind of larded jargon of psychological research. Their work stemmed from the very brass-tacks issues of practice. I became a groupie of these people, and I read everything they wrote. Then I went to some of the work on literature. There are the classic studies by I. A. Richards of how students learned literature at Cambridge. So I started to read voraciously—you know, something borrowed, something new—and I patched together a kind of approach. I read widely in historiography. I became a devotee of the philosopher of history Louis O. Mink. His *Historical Understanding* became a guide for me to the problems of interpretation. Mink wrote an essay that appeared in the journal *History and Theory* in 1961 called "The Autonomy of Historical Understanding." That piece is the most brilliant explication of historical knowing in the English language.

LUCAS: You said earlier that when you were a boy, *The Illustrated History of the United States* gave you a coherent narrative of American history. Do all kids come to their first history class with some sort of narrative in their heads, and is it worthwhile for history instructors to take that narrative into account?

WINEBURG: Absolutely. No young person who has lived through seventeen or eighteen Martin Luther King Days and Thanksgivings is lacking a narrative of beginnings, of accounting for the race problem that riddles this country, of Manifest Destiny and Western settlement, of the wars that have punctuated U.S. history. Now the chronology might be off, and these narratives would probably not suit Lynn Cheney or Gary Nash. But they are powerful narratives nonetheless. When we don't reveal the narratives that young people bring to classrooms, we are teaching to whom it may concern. And good teachers never teach to whom it may concern. Good teachers teach to Joe and to Sam and to Susan and to Paul and to Shakira. An absolutely central part of good teaching is to try to engage the narratives that learners bring to us so that, like skillful sculptors, we can move, shape, and unnerve them when necessary. Otherwise we're just putting on a patina, a layer onto something whose fundamental structure we leave untouched.

Popular and Professional History

John Lukacs

T*he Path between the Seas,* the hitherto best history of the building of the
Panama Canal, written by David McCullough, was published in 1977. In
a widely adopted and best-selling American history textbook by two Harvard
professors Freidel and Brinkley, *America in the Twentieth Century* (1982), the
bibliography lists McCullough's book with these words: "A lucid popular history of the building of the canal."

Popular history? What kind of nonsense this is. *The Path between the Seas*
was not only well written; McCullough's research, reading, and scholarship
were largely faultless. This volume represented—indeed, demonstrated—just
about all of the qualifications and the desiderata of a historian and then some
—indeed, of a professional as well as of a popular historian, by vocation;
though not an academic historian, by affiliation.

Modern historical consciousness evolved in Western Europe during the
sixteenth and seventeenth centuries. "Historian," as distinct from an annalist
or a chronicler, appears in the English language, according to the *OED,*
sometime between 1531 and 1645. Further development of (until the twentieth century, almost exclusively Western) historical consciousness occurred
in stages. During the eighteenth century, history was regarded and read as literature. During the nineteenth century, history was for the first time seen as
a science. During the twentieth century, history was often considered as a
principal social science. (I believe that in the twenty-first century, history will
become literature again: but this will not be a reversal—rather, a contrary
development: while academic history may become less and less literary, all
prose literature may become more and more historical. But I am a historian,
not a prophet.)

From *Historically Speaking* 3 (April 2002)

Back to the twentieth century, where we may detect (without much straining of our eyes) a dual development. As an expectable and natural consequence of the democratization of entire societies, the scope of historical reconstruction has broadened. This widening involved many things: the study and the occasional reconstruction of the history of majorities and not only of the ruling minorities; the widening of the area of historical study and description beyond the records of politics and of government; the adoption of methods and of materials from the other "sciences," such as sociology, geography, psychology, etc. The results have been mixed (for often they amounted to not much more than the questionable data of retrospective sociologization), but that is not my argument here. My argument is that we are still in the presence of a dual development: for this by-and-large inevitable and even commendable broadening of our historical perspective and study has occurred together with a lamentable narrowing of some of the practices of professional historianship, often to the extent that "academic" may be a more telling adjective than "professional."

Now this widening of historical study and interest in our democratic age cannot be but welcome. Let me cite one of my bêtes noires, the first edition of the *Dictionary of the French Academy,* published in 1694, which defined history as "the narration of actions and of matters worth remembering." The eighth edition, in 1935, said much of the same: "of acts, of events, of matters worth remembering." *Dignes de mémoire!* Worth remembering! What nonsense this is! Is the historian the kind of professional whose training qualifies him to tell ordinary people what is worth remembering, to label or authenticate persons or events as if they were fossil fish or pieces of rock? Is there such a thing as a person and another such thing as a historical person? Every event is a historical event; every source is (at least potentially) a historical source. History has now entered the democratic age, which simply means (the meaning is simple, though its reconstruction is complicated) that the historian must at least consider all kinds of events and all kinds of people. However—this obvious, and necessary, widening of the scope of historical knowledge and of its subjects has occurred together with a frequent narrowing of professional historianship.

In 1777 the first Ph.D. in History was granted in Göttingen. A little more than one hundred years later such degrees were granted in almost every country in Europe and in America, except for England following a little later. That the professional qualification of historianship and the concept of history as science rose together, marking the history of history during the nineteenth century, is obvious. It had much to do with the German notion of *Wissenschaft,* a term somewhat broader than the common English concept of "science," but of course there was much more to it. The merits and the achievements, many of them long lasting and still valid, of the German-inspired (though not exclusively German-discovered) Science of History were enormous. Still, more than a century later we know—or ought to know—that the strictly scientific concept and canons of history can no longer remain sacrosanct, including such notions that professional history is restricted to a study of documentary records; that such records are categorically divisible into primary and secondary sources; and that proper historical research and reconstruction will give us an absolute and incontrovertible, unchangeable and unchanging truth about this or that portion of the past.

For almost two hundred years now our knowledge of the past has been enriched (and is still being enriched) by monographs produced by serious professional historians of many kinds, even when these were (or still are) essentially meant to be written by professional historians for other professional historians, specialists in this or that portion of history. At the same time we ought to remember that during the nineteenth century, the very century when history had become professional, with many of its practitioners employed in universities, the works of many noted professional historians were bought and read by the educated public. This was so for Ranke, Treitschke, Sybel in Germany; or for Michelet and Sorel in France; this was so not only for the great nonacademic historians such as Macaulay in England, or for Tocqueville or Taine in France; this was so in the United States, too, for such different historians as Bancroft or McMaster or, somewhat later, Beard.

Even then there were historians (Burckhardt or Mommsen, for example) who recognized that history has no language and no method of its own; or that history was art as much, if not more, than science. Then, during the twentieth century, the professionalization of history proceeded apace with the bureaucratization of the profession. What happened often was not really a further separation of professional from "amateur" historians but the devolution of many professional historians into narrowly academic ones. By "narrowly" I do not mean specialists. Good specialists are what we all badly need (and not only in history); trendy and bureaucratic academics not at all. A good and honest specialist is not someone who "knows more and more about less and less." He is someone who is seriously interested in his subject, even going beyond the frontiers of his subject. The bureaucratic academic is the very opposite of that. He is less interested in history than in historianship. His primary ambition is his standing within his department and among his peers; he is ever ready to adjust not only his ideas but the theme and even the subjects of his work to what seems to be politic, respectable, or popular—within the academic or intellectual world, that is.

The harmful effects of the bureaucratization of professional historianship need not be detailed or even summed up, except perhaps to say that they involve not only questionable methods or even vocabularies but the very personalities and the characters of their practitioners. That learned men have their own petty vanities is nothing new; it should be known to all literate people (read but Johnson's "Rasselas"). But we also face, I think, a relatively new phenomenon: the unsureness, rather than the self-satisfaction of academics who wish to be properly reviewed and, on occasion, properly published in a professional journal but who, at the same time, would give their right arm to be printed or reviewed in the *New York Review of Books* or even the *New Republic*—and not at all only for commercial reasons. Something more than customary vanity is at work here. It includes the uneasy, and, as yet, hardly conscious sense within the academy that we are—surprisingly—living at a time of an unprecedented and, yes, popular interest in history.

Toward the end of the twentieth century, indeed, of the entire Modern Age there developed among the peoples of the world a phenomenon which was unexpected and unprecedented: a gross appetite for history. This appeared at the same time when traditional beliefs and habits and customs and traditional practices of education and of artistic representation were vanishing. The evidences of this prevalent and spreading appetite for history have been so multitudinous and protean that merely to list them, or to sum them up, would take many pages. They include matters such as the burgeoning of popular historical magazines, of all kinds of historical societies, of all kinds of historical programs on television and in the movies. What is even more telling: books about history and biographies now sell much more and much better than do novels—a reversal after 250 years when the novel first appeared as a form of literature. Perhaps the most remarkable evidence of this tendency may be found in the United States, whose popular ethos, the *Novus Ordo Seclorum,* had a nonhistorical or perhaps even antihistorical tinge. I cannot, at this point, and within this article, even speculate why this has been happening (except perhaps to say that it has had nothing to do with the so-called "conservative" movement, since this appetite for history amounts to something deeper than a reaction against Liberalism or Marxism). Let me only say that history is never of one piece: that currents on the surface, however oceanic looking and powerful, evolve at the same time with other, deeper currents that are flowing in different directions. And we must also consider that this, I repeat, is not a return to what happened 250 years ago when people began to be interested in history as if that were a new and interesting form of litera-ture. Those readers still belonged to the small minority of the upper and edu-cated classes, whereas now an appetite for history exists among many kinds of people in what are now increasingly classless societies.

One of the marks of this surprising and encouraging phenomenon is that we are now in the presence of something like a golden age of biography. Sev-enty years ago Harold Nicolson, a superb biographer, speculated that biog-raphy may have come to an end because of the scientific, rather than artistic, exploration of the human mind. The opposite has happened. It is not psycho-analysis but history that is now married to biography. One hundred years ago there were not many who considered biography as a form of history; it was but a form of literature, and there were not many serious historians who wrote biographies. This is now past. What is more important is the appetite of the reading public for all kinds of biographies—and equally important, the con-dition that every serious biographer in our time feels compelled to do his research and to compose his text in entire accord with the professional prac-tices of historiography.

Much of this unprecedented and impressive growth of a popular appetite for history has been ignored by the majority of academic historians. It has developed at the same time when the disappearance of history courses, not to speak of requirements, in high schools and even colleges was going on, and when the gap between academic and popular history was widening. In the *American Scholar* (Winter 1999) under the title "Teaching American History," a symposium on the National History Standards, I wrote:

> Yes, historical appetite among Americans is unprecedented and large.
> Of course it is served, and will continue to be served, by plenty of junk
> food. Of that professional historians may be aware. Of the existence
> of the appetite for history they are not.
>
>   That is the problem—the isolation of professional intellectuals,
> a largely self-made isolation that is perhaps more extreme than it was
> in the past. When the problem is nutrition, the recognition of the
> appetite comes first. Then comes the recognition and the criticism
> of junk food, which is hardly corrigible by the printing of a national
> cookbook—or even less by a pamphlet on National Nutritional Stan-
> dards with which, I am afraid, the present debate, with all of its merits,
> is concerned.

Rereading this I think that I should have written *academic,* rather than *pro-fessional* historians, for at least two reasons. There are professional historians who *do* recognize the problem, and who are capable of writing history with high professional standards and qualities at the same time when their narrative prose is, at least potentially, popular. The other reason is the existence of the works of many nonacademic historians and biographers whose lack of an academic affiliation is seldom sufficient to categorize them as being nonprofessional, or "popular." If there is a division, (and that is not always clearly ascertainable), it is not between professional and popular historians but between creative historians and academic historians, or—perhaps—between good historians and bad ones. That a good poet is someone who must have a Ph.D. in poetry is of course absurd (though, here and there, we are getting to that, too). That one must have a Ph.D. to be a good historian is less absurd: but, still. . . .

Yes, appetite is a good thing, a gift from God. But the value of things depends on their husbanding; and given human frailty, the recognition of an appetite immediately calls forth all kinds of people ready to profit from it. Yes, we are in the presence of this great and unexpected appetite for history. But we also have a host of its gross providers. And what appears, too, is the temptation of able historians to adjust (and frequently lower) their standards of work when the living comes easy. There is the recent example of Stephen Ambrose. There is the example of Barbara Tuchman, whose *The Zimmermann Telegram* was a first-rate and unexceptionable study in military and international history: but then, whatever their popular successes, her subsequent works did not quite represent such standards, until her last celebrated volume, *The March of Folly*, showed insufficient reading and a host of questionable assertions. There are the examples of some of the books of historians among us who during the last thirty years or so have successfully translated themselves from England to these shores. (Kennedy, Keegan, Schama come to mind.) I began this article by citing David McCullough's *The Path between the Seas* as a sterling example of "popular history" that was (and remains) much more than merely "popular." Yet his Truman and Adams biographies, successful as they are, and with their research following a number of professional standards, do not quite compare in their qualities with his earlier books. (Robert Ferrell's Truman biography, in my opinion, is richer and better than McCullough's—and it is half the latter's size.)

But then this is a human predicament. With the still-rising flood of all kinds of historical writing and pictorial stuff, we ought to be aware of how junk food can feed and even satisfy appetites. I am not, for a moment, arguing for the abolition of the Ph.D., or of professional or even "merely" academic historianship. I often think that the main task of academic historians, now and in the future, is to recognize and describe and point out twistings and falsifications and other mistakes and shortcomings in this or that kind of historical representation. But that kind of effort must be more than academic snobbery, more than a result of conscious (or unconscious) envy, more than a suggestive assertion that historical truth is a matter for professional historians, their restricted province. What we must recognize is that the purpose of history is the reduction of untruth. And is it not at least possible that the present appetite of all kinds of people for history may be largely due to their, perhaps hardly conscious, dissatisfaction with the large and heavy clouds of untruths hanging over the world, affecting our very lives in this age of mass democracy, of a—so-called—"Information Age"?

The Public Use of History

Jeremy Black

The public use of history has become more apparent in recent decades. Since 1945 over 120 new states have been created, each of which has had to define a new public history. At the same time, public histories in both old and new states have been, and are, contested. Far from there being any "death of the past" (J. H. Plumb) or "end of history" (Francis Fukuyama), this process is active and important, albeit at very different levels.

In 2005, for example, the discussion of nineteenth-century rural social changes created a furor in Scotland. The academic argument, advanced by Michael Fry, that these were not as harsh and disastrous as was once commonly believed was bitterly criticized by those who grounded Scottish national identity on a sense of loss and suffering, of foreign exploitation and domestic betrayal—a frequent theme around the world. Another aspect of contested public memory occurred in China, as growing academic stress on the iniquities and harshness of Mao Zedong's rule and regime clashed with the state orthodoxy that has been willing to admit to mistakes but not to a very bloody and inefficient tyranny.

Public history is a topic rich in intellectual and pedagogic possibilities, but our teaching and writing about history reflect a self-referencing fascination with the technical aspects of research and, even more, epistemologies of history. Academics see themselves as the drivers of historical assessments. But changes in the public use of history are crucial to the general understanding of the past, and these developments stem largely from current political shifts and pressures. Thus, for instance, the recent collapse of communism across

From *Historically Speaking* 7 (May/June 2006)

much of Eurasia was followed by a recovery of non- and anticommunist themes, topics, and approaches. In Estonia, for example, it became possible —indeed appropriate—to emphasize the destructiveness of Soviet conquest and occupation and to discuss both the many victims as well as those who resisted. It will be instructive to see how far the same process occurs in post-Castro Cuba.

The role of public history in politics is significant: issues of national identity and political legitimation are central. The context is often a long-term one. When, for example, members of the Polish Parliament from two populist parties occupied the chamber in 2002, they were criticized for reviving what were seen as the anarchic traditions of the old Polish Commonwealth. This was a very charged comparison. Anarchic impulses were seen as a significant factor in the weakness that led to the partitions of Poland in 1772–95.

Public history is in large part a product of broader patterns of social experience, such as, shifts in collective memory, and of social change, such as, the rise of literacy. These patterns of social experience create narratives and analyses that are somewhat different from those that predominate in Western academic circles. For example, there is a tension between popular and academic approaches over the role of contingency and human agency. Popular narratives rely upon the drama of human agency: people make history. Drawing frequently on the social sciences, academic historians often emphasize the structural aspects of situations—necessity can be purchased at the expense of choice and contingency. Such tensions can be seen in the differing response to shifts in academic historiography. For example, although the *Annales* approach to history was highly influential in the academy, it has had very little impact on popular views. Similarly the public has shown limited appetite for the more fractured, complex discussions of the past produced by Western scholars. Another major divide between public interest and academic fashion relates to objectivity. Popular history assumes the possibility of objectivity or, at the minimum, detachment, something many academic historians influenced by the "linguistic turn" in historiography consider epistemologically naïve.

In short, academic history is guided by an idealist approach, one that regards issues of historical theory and method, such as, the recovery of truth or the creation of "truths," as more significant than what is taught in classrooms or published in popular works. Linked to this is a hierarchical structuring of relations within the historical profession. Those who focus on historiography claim what is akin to a higher purpose compared to those colleagues who work on narrative or empirical topics.

There is also the more general question of the reputation of academic historians outside the profession. In recent decades the idea of the intellectual, the practice of free speech, and the institutional autonomy of universities combined to give academic historians a measure of independence. But this is under challenge in the West. Aside from political and governmental pressures, both in evidence in Britain, there are also those that stem directly from popular interests. This is readily apparent in the case of religious history, where academic discussion of key aspects of Christian history has been swamped by the outpourings stemming from Dan Brown's *Da Vinci Code.*

Irrespective of this and in contrast to the self-image of the modern Western academic, the role of the academic as the servant of the state is more important across much of the world. It is likely that this role will become more significant in the future, especially in East and South Asia, where academics depend on public funding and generally operate under the threat of censorship. They work within a context in which the goal and content of most historical research and teaching are very sensitive: history is a crucial aspect of nationalism. Witness the recent controversies in China and Japan. Advance word that the 2005 edition of *The New History Textbook* created by the nationalist Japanese Society for Textbook Reform would remove "any reference to matters associated with . . . 'dark history' [issues, such as, the comfort women or the rape of Nanjing] that might make Japanese schoolchildren uncomfortable" prompted angry Chinese to stone the Japanese Consulate in Shanghai.

This raises the question of whether the relationship between academic and public history in the West is typical for the rest of the world—indeed whether there can be global criteria for historiography. This issue can be clearly seen in debates over the relationship between nationalism and objectivity. Scholars in the West divide over the possibility of recovering the past, but they generally desire to avoid nationalistic partisanship. That, however, means little in many states across the world, where partisanship and national identity are intertwined.

At the same time, it would be woefully mistaken to imagine that these are only issues in the developing world. The controversy over the National History Standards, and, indeed, the unease that lay behind the establishment of the Historical Society in 1997, reflected the contentiousness of historical content and methods in *both* popular and academic circles. In Europe there is considerable contention over the historical nature of its identity and culture. This is far from being only of academic interest. The issue is very much to the forefront as Turkish accession to the European Union is debated. This directly relates to such questions as the role of Christianity in European identity and the nature of Turkish development in the twentieth century. The latter has been particularly contentious in the case of Turkish willingness to confront the Armenian massacres, while there has also been European criticism of the nature of Atatürk's regime.

In European settlement societies, particularly Australia, Canada, and New Zealand and, to a lesser extent, the Andean States and the United States, there is also the question of how "first peoples" were treated. This was very much an issue in the New Zealand general election of 2005, with the center-right opposition National Party criticizing what its leader in 2005 termed the "grievance industry" centered on Maori land claims. He promised an end to the numerous claims and the reversal of any legislation granting special privileges to Maoris. What is termed "black armband" history with reference to the treatment of the Aborigines has also proved very contentious and divisive in Australia, and it has become more pronounced in recent years.

Global demographics will affect public history around the world. Ninety-five percent of the world's population increase is taking place in the developing world, and it is there that the pressures to provide a readily comprehensible public history will be most acute. It is interesting to note, for example, how Indian politicians, both from the Congress government and the BJP (Bharatiya Janata Party) opposition, faced criticism as they addressed traditional suppositions about the unhelpful nature of British imperial rule as well as the role of Pakistan. In 2005 the willingness of Prime Minister Manmohan Singh to offer a good-and-bad account of British rule caused controversy.

Governments in developing countries will need to develop unifying national myths, especially as the liberation myths used in the immediate postcolonial period become less potent. A variety of factors make this more urgent: the volatility of societies in the developing world, with the relatively large percentage of their populations under the age of twenty-five; the disruptive impact of urbanization and industrialization; the breakdown of patterns of deference and social control; and pressures on established networks, identities, and systems of explanation. There is also the challenge posed by particular constructions of ethnicity and religion within these states and how they interact with historicized notions of identity and development. We need to devote more attention in historiography courses to the process of forging new public histories in the developing world. It will be both interesting and important to see how dynamic societies come to grips with their recent and more distant past. And this will probably be the most significant aspect of historiography over the next century.

PART 2

Postmodernism: Three Views

Postmodernism and the Truth of History

C. Behan McCullagh

The great contribution of postmodern thought to our assessment of human knowledge has been to remind us that our knowledge is generally couched in language, so it does not mirror the world as we believe most of our perceptions do. Our knowledge is constructed from elements of our culture, employing concepts and forms of argument that we have learned and believe to be appropriate. Our descriptions of the world reflect our interests, values, and purposes, so they are not perfectly impartial and complete accounts of the subjects they describe. They seldom capture every detail of the subjects we describe, so they are, in that sense, almost always incomplete. Furthermore, the meanings of the words we use, which depend upon their relations to other words, cannot be fixed with any precision, so that the descriptions are always vague.

These are true and important points, and they have been used by some to cast doubt upon the truth of historical descriptions. Frank Ankersmit, Beverley Southgate, and Alun Munslow, for example, have all denied that general interpretations of past events can be true for these reasons, though they have, rather inconsistently, allowed that descriptions of particular historical events can be true. Robert Berkhofer Jr. and Keith Jenkins have gone further, arguing that when descriptions of particular historical facts are embedded in an interpretative narrative, they fail to provide us with reliable information about the past.[1]

If these facts make narrative interpretations of the past unbelievable, then they make descriptions of particular events incredible as well. Why on earth should we think that historical knowledge, a culturally bound linguistic construction in the present, bears any particular relation to past events at all?

The trouble is, that if we insist upon skepticism toward statements of particular facts about the past, we will have to abandon almost all the beliefs we live by. In practice we have developed very reliable methods of distinguishing statements about the world that are worthy of belief from those that are not. To defend the credibility of singular descriptions, we should study those methods and carefully consider their significance.[2]

To put it briefly, although we cannot perceive events in the past, we can draw reliable inferences about many of them on the basis of observable evidence available to us. Logically speaking, historical inferences form an explanatory chain: we explain our perceptual experiences as caused by material things we perceive; we explain many of those material things, such as letters and buildings, as the product of human activity; and we explain that human activity as a response to a situation faced by the agent or agents in their world at the time. These explanations rely not just upon our perceptions but also upon other particular and general facts we already believe to be true. But notice that the historical knowledge that results from these chains of inference is not justified simply on grounds of coherence. It is based upon, and controlled by, the observations of evidence, which form its foundation. Sometimes the general knowledge that mediates explanations is contested. For instance, historians often hold strong but differing opinions about the relative importance of ideas, cultural practices, economic interests, and the desire for power in determining human behavior. But the number of uncontested facts inferred about the past on the basis of observed evidence is enormous.

This pattern of inference from perceptions is similar to that by which we sometimes decide what exists in the world around us. Suppose you see a perfect flower in a vase, it could be real or artificial. To check, you feel and smell it, and when you find it feels like plastic and has no scent, you decide it is artificial: that best explains the evidence of your senses. We are only aware of the inferences involved when we are uncertain as to how to interpret our perceptual experiences. Normally the inference is quite automatic. For example, we instantly assume people believe what they avow and desire what they ask for, since that is normally the case. But sometimes, on the basis of what we already know, this seems unlikely. If a man were to say that the famous urinal displayed by Marcel Duchamp is beautiful, one would wonder whether he was being ironic and question him further.

Why should we believe that the conclusions of such chains of inference truly describe the past, or the present for that matter? Obviously we cannot check them by observing what happened in the past, and even if we could, we would have to explain those observations! What we have to realize is that our knowledge of the world, past and present, is entirely a construction of our minds, based on our perceptual experiences but framed with concepts and words derived from our culture and inferred according to patterns of inference believed to yield reliable conclusions. It seems that what we are aiming at ideally in reasoning about what exists is an account that will explain all the perceptual experiences we could possibly have. But what does it mean to call such an ideal explanation "true"? I suggest that it means two things, first, that no better explanation of all possible experiences is likely to be found, and second, that the world is such as to produce all the experiences upon which the ideal theory is based, were the appropriate people in the appropriate places to experience them. In calling the conclusion of a historical inference true, we mean that it would form part of an ideal explanation of all experiences of the world.

While some exponents of postmodern philosophy are incautiously ready to accept the truthfulness of particular facts about the past, they are all recklessly willing to deny that historical interpretations can possibly be true. In this they faithfully follow their mentor Ankersmit, whom Munslow esteems as "the most significant historical thinker today."[3] Ankersmit has argued that historical interpretations are created by historians and correspond to no reality in the past.[4] All have assumed that historical interpretations cannot be true, because they reflect the aesthetic, moral, and political preferences of the historians who produce them.

This, however, is a fallacy. The fact that a historian identifies an interesting pattern among historical events does not mean the pattern did not exist. Many histories describe the growth or decline of an institution, such as, the Roman Empire, or cycles in the fortunes of something, such as, an economy. In such ways they interpret large numbers of particular historical events, whose occurrence has been established on the basis of evidence. If such patterns fairly describe the subjects to which they are attributed, then we are justified in saying that they truly existed, just as we can say that a tree really grows as its cells multiply and its branches wave in the wind as they are tossed to and fro. The fact that historians select such patterns because they find them interesting does not imply that they do not exist.

In the context of a discussion of the objectivity of historical interpretations, it is worth drawing attention to a feature of interpretations that postmodernists have studiously ignored, namely their adequacy in answering the questions that elicited them.

In times gone by, historians, particularly those writing in the nineteenth century (whose work Hayden White analyzed[5]), were prone to write narratives for moral or political purposes, structuring them more or less as they wished. But professional historians today seek greater understanding of the past and put precise questions to the information they have gathered about particular events. These questions reflect their interests, but they also provide constraints upon the narratives that result.[6]

Sometimes historians set themselves the task of describing and explaining the growth or decline of an institution. For instance, Robert Fawtier sets out to describe and explain the growth of the power of the Capetian kings of France between 987 and 1328. The power of the Capetians depended upon the extent of their estates, the number of their vassals, and the efficiency of their administration. Consequently his narrative history plots the changes in these things between those years, explaining each as it goes. The only room for choice in this process lies in the degree of detail one chooses to offer, which depends upon the size of the book one wishes to write.

Certainly one can ask other questions about the Capetians, according to one's interests. But the answers to those questions are by no means arbitrary. One could ask, for instance, about their influence upon the cultural and intellectual life of France, as Robert Fawtier does in one chapter of his book.[7] Here there seems more room for choice, but once again the question limits the direction of historians' responses. It prompts them to consider intellectual inquiry, art, and language. Under royal patronage the University of Paris eventually became preeminent in France, and the Gothic style in art and architecture became widely adopted. The use of the language of the north, langue d'oïl, by the royal administration perhaps contributed to its becoming the dominant language of the country. The selection and arrangement of facts in a historical narrative are often constrained by the question it is designed to answer.

Biographers invariably explore the beliefs and aspirations that shaped their subjects' behavior. Sometimes they are able to identify one set of ideas that inspired a person, as when Randall Bennett Woods explained that Senator J. W. Fulbright's various policies were based upon the conviction that progress would occur when people understood the world and possessed the freedom to act rationally within it. His Fulbright Scholarship scheme stemmed from this conviction. Sometimes the subject of a biography is more complex, and there is room for disagreement about the person's main motivation. Once the central character of a subject has been established, the narrative of that person's life may be written to illustrate the general interpretation of his or her character. But if it fails to include and make sense of major activities in the life of the subject, it will be judged inadequate.

Some histories are written to explain why certain major events occurred. There are two kinds of explanation that commonly interest historians. They are often interested in the events that increased the probability of the event in the circumstances, tracing its origin by providing an account of its genesis, in what I call a *genetic explanation.* They are also frequently interested in why the event in question occurred rather than another event, which seemed equally possible at some point of time. This is to ask for a *contrastive explanation,* looking for conditions that made the actual outcome more probable than a specific possible alternative. For instance, in explaining why the North won the American Civil War, one could describe the events that brought their victory about, as well as point out conditions, such as their superior resources and leadership, that made a Northern victory more probable than a Southern one.

Very often the histories written by academic historians, such as those just mentioned, address questions that severely limit the form they can take. These questions provide the standard of adequacy against which the histories can be measured.

Postmodernists, by drawing attention to the subjective and cultural sources of historical knowledge, have concluded that such knowledge is nothing but a personal and cultural construction, providing us with no reliable information about the past. In fact historians often provide credible narratives and interpretations of the past and give plausible analyses of what happened in response to the questions people ask about past events.

NOTES

1. F. R. Ankersmit, *Narrative Logic: A Semantic Analysis of the Historian's Language* (Leiden: Martinus Nijhoff, 1983); Beverley Southgate, *Postmodernism in History: Fear or Freedom?* (London: Routledge, 2003); Alun Munslow, *The New History;* Robert E. Berkhofer Jr., *Beyond the Great Story: History as Text and Discourse* (Cambridge, Mass.: Harvard University Press, 1995); and Keith Jenkins, *Refiguring History: New Thoughts on an Old Discipline* (London: Routledge, 2003).

2. This I have attempted to do most succinctly in my recent book *The Logic of History* (London: Routledge, 2003).

3. Munslow, *New History,* 166.

4. Ankersmit, *Narrative Logic.* He sometimes wavers from this view slightly; see also C. Behan McCullagh, "Bias in Historical Description, Interpretation, and Explanation," *History and Theory* 39, no. 1 (2000): 58.

5. Hayden White, *Metahistory: The Historical Imagination in Nineteenth-Century Europe* (Baltimore: Johns Hopkins University Press, 1975).

6. I have analyzed and illustrated common forms of these patterns of interpretation in *The Truth of History* (London: Routledge, 1998).

7. Robert Fawtier, *The Capetian Kings of France: Monarchy and Nation, 987–1328,* trans. L. Butler and R. J. Adam (New York: Macmillan, 1964), chap. 12.

Postmodernism and Historical Inquiry

Spoiled for Choice?

Beverley Southgate

For me, postmodernism definitively arrived on December 12, 1997. On that day the London *Times* reported that Prime Minister Tony Blair had gone beyond the bounds of conventional diplomatic generosity by offering the Irish negotiator Gerry Adams nothing less than "a choice of history." For a mere mortal to claim to have such dispensations in his gift may sound extraordinarily hubristic to historians brought up to assert their own unique rights over a past, the nature of which it was for them, and only them, to determine. But for those attempting to assess the implications of postmodernism for historical inquiry, Blair's offer does at least make a start. And as we grope our way through something of a conceptual fog, the key word *choice* does provide one useful beacon.

What Blair implied with his offer of historical choice was that, while the events of the past (with all their anger and frustration and violence) are undoubtedly there—or rather here, in our present—what actually matters is not their existence, their presence per se, but rather our responses to them. We can look at them, respond to them, remember them, either in such a way as will lead to further disruption or one that will facilitate reconciliation. What Adams had, and what historians have, is a choice of narrative—a choice of the way to "emplot" those past events or put them in a story that leads from them, through our present, and forward to the future.

From *Historically Speaking* 6 (January/February 2005). For comments on an earlier draft, I am grateful to Dennis Brown and John Ibbett.

That seems to me to get to the heart of what postmodernism implies for historical inquiry—where *postmodernism* represents an attempt to theorize and make some intellectual sense of, our actual situation in postmodernity; and *postmodernity* I take to be simply a chronological category, with disputable boundaries like any other, but one that enables us at least provisionally to locate ourselves in the ever-rolling stream of time.

Thus tentatively located, our condition seems to me to display a number of interlocking features, which can themselves be seen as the culmination of historical trends. And the narrative net that I cast over that past catches at least the following in its mesh: first, a post-Copernican decentering—an enforced realization that I personally am neither static nor the center of the universe and that indeed there is no single or static center from which either nature or the past can be definitively viewed, assessed, described, and re-presented; second, that a skeptical philosophy, originating in classical antiquity, revived as a central ingredient of early modern thought, and newly regenerated, reminds us of humans' inherent inadequacy—physical and intellectual—in any pursuit of "truth," whether scientific or historical; third, that linguistic studies, going back again to Plato but powerfully revived and reinforced in the twentieth century, clarify our essential inability to describe the external world (including nature and the past) without deficiency; and fourth, that following the death of God, so chillingly announced by Nietzsche, there can be no reliance on absolute foundations, whether in religion itself or science or history.

Taken together, this shoal of elements serves for me to characterize our life in postmodernity (though doubtless there are smaller fry that have eluded us). These elements are evident not just as theories *intellectually* maintained but as feelings *existentially* experienced: that's simply our lot in the twenty-first century, our cultural inheritance. And not even historians can escape that; not even they are exempt. Devoted they may be to inquiry into the past, preferring perhaps, like Petrarch, to commune with illustrious forbears rather than degenerate contemporaries, but they'll find in that past no secure refuge or bolt-hole from the present; for the validity of even such supposedly rigid chronological distinctions as past and present and future has been rendered suspect, as they seep one into another.

Historians, then, confront a subject that's been dislocated and destabilized, a subject that, if it is to survive at all, has to function as a decentered, foundationless, relativistic, linguistically problematic, endlessly ambiguous enterprise, where choice is no optional extra—not just a possibility in the gift of Tony Blair or anyone else—but at its very core. The central question thus becomes whether historians and their subjects are in some way *spoiled* by that choice—spoiled in the sense now of being undermined, invalidated, rendered obsolete or whether they are not rather presented with a new and vital role. For it's surely one of the paradoxes of our time, that just as the greatest need is felt for a history to give meaning and a sense of direction, the authority of history as guide is lost.

What in particular has come under question is the possibility of any such unitary truth as that to which historical inquiry has traditionally aspired. Truth has long been the Holy Grail, to whose quest historians have been consecrated. The first requirement for any historian, as Ranke confirms, is their "pure love of truth."[1] Further, hope of its attainment has always depended on ascetic renunciation of their human selves. For, as with the natural sciences, this quest has a quasi-theological dimension. And like medieval knights and Victorian scientists, historians have pursued their objects—in their case what "really happened" in the past—with religious fervor and intensity. Then, with the vision of that reality granted in exchange for self-denial and personal detachment, historians—still disembodied—could reveal their truth to mortals. Applauded by Lord Acton as being "seen at his best when he does not appear,"[2] the invisible "narrator from nowhere" could impersonally dispense properly "balanced" judgments on the past.

The long-lived identification of historical truth with *the* correct representation of the past has now perished. Truth, it is clear, cannot be absolute, unambiguous, unquestionable, or static but can perhaps be better seen as part of an intellectual (and experiential) structure that we have, however provisionally or unconsciously, agreed to accept. Even for professional historians, after all, a particular sort of "truth" was chosen—in their case, a scientific-historical truth that was to be contrasted with another more "romantic" style which came to be identified with amateurs. Just as Turner's depiction of St. Benedetto in Venice was recognized by Ruskin as being, though "without one single accurate detail," in some sense "true" in spirit to the place, so J. A. Froude commended Shakespeare's poetic plays as "the most perfect English history." And Carlyle's endorsement of Sir Walter Scott's novels is, of course, well known: for him, the very works that inspired Ranke with such repugnance for their "subjective" intrusions, embodied truths that often lay hidden in more "objective" histories.

That distinction between poetic, novelistic truth and truth as revealed by historians dates back at least to Thucydides and Aristotle: the former defined his own scientific history by contrast with the romances of his poetic predecessor; the latter followed his Platonic master's voice, marking out history's terrain again by contrast with that of poetry. The point here is that in each case there was a self-consciously adopted choice of what was to count as "truth"; though with those ancient distinctions long since enshrined in disciplinary structures, any notion of such choice has long since been forgotten. But now, in postmodernity, the possibility—indeed, the necessity—of choice recurs, as the foundations, authority, necessity, and naturalness of our previously chosen type of truth come under scrutiny, and we are forced now to realize that, even in historical inquiry, self-serving protestations of ideological aloofness reflect nothing other than (conscious or unconscious) wishful thinking.

It's small wonder, then, that postmodernism has been so strongly resisted. Acton's self-denying ordinance has been widely adopted as a corollary of properly scientific study and has well suited a priestly caste fired with idealistic ambition to hunt down its form of truth. For choice, almost universally applauded in our consumption-oriented times, proves in this context highly problematic. Historians are expected to reveal what's there, already inscribed in the past, not to choose what meaning (and so what narrative) to impose upon it.

Besides, it's a long-established paradox that we tend to flee in terror from the exercise of a freedom that, before its attainment, might have served as our goal; the institutionalized, long accustomed to having choice taken out of their hands, do not take well to having that responsibility thrust back upon them. And a main problem here is a lack of any criterion that might facilitate or enable such choice; without those externally validated standards of which by definition (in postmodernity) we are now deprived, how can we ever decide? We are surely faced here with our own consciousness of aporia—with that inescapable impasse, the recognition of which has been seen as actually serving to define the postmodern condition. With the dissolution of the rules and standards and frameworks by which we had previously ordered the world, we are confronted by an incipient chaos that threatens us at levels not only intellectual but existential, too.

This is not of course an altogether new phenomenon. Seventeenth-century writers, faced with parallel challenges to their own intellectual ordering, responded to newly revived Pyrrhonian skepticism with an angst far removed from the ataraxia (freedom from stress) envisaged by that philosophy's founder. The Platonist Joseph Mede, we are told, found that his skeptical questioning "rendered all things so unpleasant to him, that his Life became uncomfortable"; and it was only "by the mercy of God [that] he . . . made his way out of these troublesome Labyrinths"; and Henry More suffered from similar disorientation as he came to question even the validity of mathematics: "Nor whence, nor who I am, poor Wretch! know I," he wrote in an autobiographical poem significantly entitled "Aporia." "Nor yet, O Madness! Whither I must goe."[3]

Such angst may resonate for us in our own intellectual and cultural transition. Barbara Herrnstein Smith has described the "bodily distress"—the "impression of inescapable noise or acute disorder, a rush of adrenalin, sensations of alarm, a sense of unbalance or chaos, residual feelings of nausea and anxiety"—that results from having one's fundamental and hitherto deeply held beliefs challenged.[4] So we need not be surprised by some historians' emotional reactions to the cognitive dissonance to which they are currently exposed. At the very point of realization of the undecidability of the decisions they are required to make, historians are nonetheless compelled to choose, to exercise their freedom and determine for themselves what forms their histories will take. And as they endeavor personally to negotiate the evident chaos of the past, they may, with earlier disciplinary markers now withdrawn, find it hard to see a clear way forward (or backward).

Perhaps, however, that very lack of clarity can be construed as a virtue: blurred edges might better suit our times than those Manichaean-style distinctions—true or false, fact or fiction, good or evil, friend or foe, with us or against—which currently divide the world into dogma-touting partisans. It's their certainty—the fanatical conviction (on both sides) of their own rightness—to which history might properly provide some antidote. For where past histories supplied those progressive narratives that led determinedly from dark to light, consolidating an oh-so-desirable present in which we were oh-so-happy to be, what may be needed now, in our problematic present, are rather histories that investigate alternatives—histories that question the seeming inevitability and necessity of what has come to be accounted natural, necessary, and constitutive of "reality."

That brings us back to the question of truth, for however much we question the validity (or even meaningfulness) of such a concept, it seems to be one that is hard to dispense with altogether. Whether in historical inquiry, or in life more generally, we need perhaps some goal toward which to strive, some light to which to steer—even if all the while acknowledging that that end light is always shifting and elusive, never finally attainable. So that our quest, not least in history, becomes a never-ending process, a journey without final destination; and an important function for historical study itself might be to clarify and to confirm just that.

For history, after all, was originally conceived as an *inquiry*. And as such, its nature is to be ongoing, ever provoking new visions and fresh appraisals. Indeed, historians might even, like some writers of fiction, resist the allure of imposing arbitrary closure and deliberately leave their endings open and their readers with a choice. In that way they would at least do more justice to the multiplicity of outcomes known to have been possible. For there is, as Jonathan Clark has recently argued,[5] some merit in the consideration of counterfactuals, those paths that we declined to take, but could and might have taken. It's by viewing such hypothetical alternatives that we recognize the contingency of the routes we did choose. It could, in other words, have all been different: history does not have its inbuilt course, however imposed, but has its course determined by human actors. And by seeing that our forbears had a choice, we might, as Clark suggests, be less inclined to see ourselves as caught up in history's seemingly inevitable sweep and come to recognize our own ability to choose and change our future.

NOTES

1. Leopold von Ranke, "On the Character of Historical Science" (written ca. 1830), in *The Theory and Practice of History,* ed. Georg G. Iggers and Konrad von Moltke (Indianapolis: Bobbs-Merrill, 1973), 39.

2. Lord Acton, *Lectures on Modern History* (London: Macmillan, 1906; London: Fontana, 1960), 27.

3. Joseph Mede, *The Works,* ed. J. Worthington, 2 vols. (London: n.p., 1664), 1:iii; Richard Ward, *The Life of the Learned and Pious Dr. Henry More* (London: Printed and sold by Joseph Downing, 1710), 10–11.

4. Barbara Herrnstein Smith, *Belief and Resistance: Dynamics of Contemporary Intellectual Controversy* (Cambridge, Mass.: Harvard University Press, 1997), xiv.

5. J. C. D. Clark, *Our Shadowed Present: Modernism, Postmodernism, and History* (London: Atlantic, 2003).

Postmodernism and Historiography

Willie Thompson

The theoretical origins of postmodernism are primarily located in the post-structuralist philosophy that emerged in France during the later 1960s and blossomed in the 1970s. At the end of the decade the initially separate concepts of postmodernism and poststructuralism coalesced, the critical text in this regard being Jean-François Lyotard's *La Condition Postmoderne: report sur le savoir,* appearing in 1979. In it he defined postmodernism as an "incredulity towards metanarrative."

In the historiographical context, while debts are acknowledged to writers such as Jacques Lacan (psychoanalyst), Hayden White (historian of ideas), Jacques Derrida (philosopher/critic), unquestionably the principal influence has been Michel Foucault (1926–84). Foucault always denied being a postmodernist or poststructuralist and indeed ridiculed anyone who described him in these terms, but that may have been no more than a postmodern joke; nobody has done more to establish postmodernism as an intellectual presence. Foucault, always working within a linguistic framework and a concept of all-pervasive power relations constituted through discourse (it was he who popularized the term in that sense), surveyed a series of broad themes, such as, madness, medicine, social science, penal regimes, and sexuality, and had interesting things to say on all of them as well as much of dubious value. His publishers have claimed him as the most influential thinker of the twentieth century, and he has been the principal source of inspiration to historians of a postmodern sensibility, as well as to those who do not accept the validity of his approach but have found useful insights in his writings.

From *Historically Speaking* 6 (January/February 2005)

Postmodernism as we have come to know it can therefore be treated appropriately as the product of a great disillusion: disillusion with science both social and physical, disillusion with the idea of historical progress, disillusion with the possibility of far-reaching social change. Its attraction was enhanced greatly by the dramatic collapse of the Soviet-style regimes, polities that purported (however falsely) to embody such ideas and aspirations.

Frederic Jameson has defined postmodernism as the "cultural logic of late capitalism"; the cultural logic of social despair might be more fitting. It could not fail to make an impact on historiography, which is after all our source of knowledge about the past circumstances that enable judgment to be made on whether or not this is a postmodern age and whether all "metanarratives" really are discredited. It is certainly too early as yet to evaluate its full impact on historical studies, yet without question it has stimulated widespread, heated, and often ferocious discussion, while the approaches it recommends —or at least some of them—have been used in serious historiographical work. The number of published texts existing today either in advocacy of historiographical postmodernism or in critique of it or indeed influenced by its outlook would constitute a most formidable bibliography.

Not for nothing is the postmodernist outlook in general known as the "linguistic turn." It is no accident that the approach originated in and has been shaped by literary theory; literary and critical theory can indeed be regarded as its seedbed and stronghold. Literary creations (and their cognates in other media) are not subject to the constraints that have traditionally applied to representational reconstructions of actualities past or present. The point of imaginative creations is that within them the imagination can roam freely, constrained if at all only by the rules of the genre. The television cartoon strip *South Park* is a fine example of authentic postmodernism in popular culture, for it contains a character who is killed in every episode and reappears as large as life in the next in order to be killed all over again. This kind of thing is not permitted in historiographical discourse—but then, we may ask the seemingly obvious question, why not? Is it simply the arbitrary rule of that particular genre? Most (though not all) spokespersons for historiographical postmodernism would avoid such a conclusion and acknowledge that historical events did in some sense occur independently of their representations and are unalterable; that the historian's requirement to respect the historical record is not pure convention. What would be asserted, nonetheless, is that, since (it is claimed) there is no intrinsic connection between language and what language is about (in technical jargon, the signifier and the referent), it is impossible to establish explanations, understandings, and interpretations in a way that one can be regarded as in some sense better or worse than others. Historiography, apart from the bare bones of the chronicle, must therefore be treated as rhetoric, and the postmodernist agenda is self-confessedly to blur or abolish the boundaries between historical explanation and imaginative literature. Hayden White argues that every historical text of consequence begins with a "poetic act." Undoubtedly the objective is nothing less than to work a revolution in historical studies and render obsolete every tenet of historical methodology accepted prior to the linguistic turn.

It might be imagined that an approach that has aroused such a degree of interest and inspired a mass of theoretical and applied writing will certainly have something worth saying, and such a view is not altogether to be discounted. The following insights into historical study can be credited to postmodernism.

It is generally (though doubtless not universally) accepted that as a result of postmodernism's influence, historians have to be more attentive to linguistic and semantic matters. Rhetoric and phraseology require diligent examination. Not all would agree. Norman Hampson writes, "To suggest that, on the whole, the [French] revolutionary orators said what they said in the sense in which they meant it, is to confess oneself a very dull dog indeed. I remain impenitent." This robust declaration has a lot of appeal, yet in reality matters are not so simple, as indeed the author himself acknowledges a few lines later: "How things are presented is not without importance."[1]

Growing out of the greater sensitivity to "how things are presented," certain concepts and categories of discourse associated with the postmodern temper and one writer in particular, Michel Foucault, have proved useful to historians working in the area of the human sciences, especially those of medicine, psychiatry, and penology. With his emphasis on power relations formed by discourse, Foucault exposed the unpalatable and coercive underside of the humanitarian advances in these fields during the past two centuries. And though a lot of his claims may be refuted in detail, understanding of this area will never again look the same as it did before he wrote.

In a more general sense, arising from its emphasis on language and discourse, historiographical postmodernism has opened up new areas of investigation, above all that of cultural relations and processes. It has also helped to emphasize and give expression to the realization of the late twentieth century that the "grand narratives" of progress and advancement in economic, social, political, and cultural spheres stand on no sound basis. In other words, it has in the past been very easy for historians unthinkingly to allow themselves to fall into the teleologies—liberal, Marxist, or whatever—that have been attached to modernity; the postmodern turn does help to alert historians to this sort of carelessness.

There are historians who are self-proclaimed adherents of postmodern values and who write admirable history. A list of the most distinguished would include names such as Gareth Stedman Jones, Joan Wallach Scott, or Patrick Joyce, to which various others could be added. In relation to this however, two points can be made. In the first place a number of them, Joan Scott in particular, tend to leave postmodernist theory behind when they write history. If, for example, Scott's article on the manipulation of statistical information concerning the Parisian occupational structure of 1847–48 were to be read in ignorance of the author's name, it would be assumed to have been written by a methodologically orthodox historian of a Marxist temper.[2]

In the second place—and this applies particularly to the postmodernist historians of nineteenth-century Britain—their historical perspective is deliberately restricted in scope, which channels their research toward concern with representational and political/cultural questions. A similar orientation can be identified in the historical journals influenced by postmodernist thinking: their focus tends to be upon the forms of representation demonstrated in particular historical episodes rather than the actualities of such matters as living and dying, subsistence or the lack of it, oppression or physical resistance to it.

Moreover the gains associated with postmodern historiography and theory have been made at a very considerable cost, namely a distortion of the relationship between representation and the objects of representation. Postmodern historical theory (setting aside its application to other areas) is permeated with severe logical flaws. These include willful refusal to understand the nature of evidence, likewise the relationship between evidence and conclusion and the concept of scales of validity ranging from refutation to practical certainty. The tendency is to collapse reality into representation and to ignore the consideration that while reality is inexhaustible and can only ever be partially represented, representation itself is of a different ontological character. This is why postmodern historiographical theory is laid open to charges of wanting to obliterate the distinctions between historical and fictional accounts; of advocating a posture of relativist skepticism toward *all* historical interpretations, be they of trivial personal actions or of the Holocaust. Because an object, event, or process can only be represented and understood by means of a discursive construct, it does not follow that therefore it *is* a discursive—still less a fictional—construct.

There are even wilder postmodernist shores reached by some of the school's historical theorists, though, to be fair, few of the historians influenced by the trend have made landfall there. If the agenda of attenuating the distinction between historical and imaginative texts is taken seriously and emphasis laid on emplotment, rhetoric, and style in place of the ostensible content, then there is no intrinsic reason why the text should adhere to the norms of literary realism but instead, under the inspiration of Jacques Derrida, may plunge into the "differential movement of language" in which words never have fixed meanings but are open to the endless play of *différance;* so that historiography is assimilated not merely to literature but indeed to abstract poetry.

A further weakness of the postmodern view of historiography is what may be termed its intellectual and disciplinary imperialism, a strident insistence emanating from its practitioners that this is the *only* manner in which history should be written both in form and in subject—all else is outdated, empiricist, positivist, and totalizing (even totalitarian).

Postmodernist enthusiasts aggressively declare that their interpretation constitutes the foundations of a new intellectual universe and direct an intimidating rhetoric against historians who decline to accept the axiom of its superiority (although the majority of these remain obstinate infidels despite the considerable impact that postmodern missionaries have achieved). Closely related to the imperialist ambition noted here is the habit of arguing by assertion rather than evidence. It may be remarked that the fundamental propositions of postmodernist thought concerning the relation of language and discourse and representation to reality are incapable of being demonstrated: either one finds them convincing or one doesn't. One may even find in them echoes of the Hermetic tradition (hermeneutics, though a separate activity, is after all central to postmodernism), which attributed mystical or magical powers to words and metaphor.

Nevertheless, even historians most vehemently opposed to the postmodern disposition will acknowledge with greater or lesser willingness that its adherents have produced some useful insights (even Arthur Marwick accepts this in the case of Foucault). The problem is that the proponents of the style have chosen to regard these insights as the key to the historiographical universe. More likely it would be truer to suggest that in due course the useful elements of their contribution will be digested into mainstream historiography, and their more outrageous claims quietly forgotten.

NOTES

1. Norman Hampson, *Saint-Just* (Oxford: Blackwell, 1991), ii.
2. Joan Wallach Scott, "A Statistical Representation of Work: La Statistique de l'industrie à Paris 1847–1848," in *Gender and the Politics of History* (New York: Columbia University Press, 1999), 113–38.

PART 3

Assessing Counterfactuals

Telling It Like It Wasn't

Richard J. Evans

What if William the Conqueror had lost the battle of Hastings? What if Martin Luther had been burned at the stake in 1521? What if the British had managed to hold on to the American colonies in 1776? What if Napoleon had won the battle of Waterloo? What if Lenin had not died prematurely in 1924 but had lived on for another twenty years? What if Germany had succeeded in conquering Britain in 1940?

Imagining what might have happened is always fun. A very diverse range of serious and distinguished historians has indulged in this pastime, including G. M. Trevelyan, Conrad Russell, John Vincent, Hugh Trevor-Roper, Geoffrey Parker, Alistair Horne, Theodore Rabb, Andrew Roberts, Robert Katz, William H. McNeill, and many others. In recent years it has become increasingly fashionable to engage in such speculation, and collections of essays have appeared with titles such as *If I Had Been . . . Ten Historical Fantasies,* edited by Daniel Snowman in 1979; *For Want of a Horse,* edited by Niall Ferguson in 1997; and *What If?—The World's Foremost Military Historians Imagine What Might Have Been,* edited by Robert Cowley in 1998, and so successful that a second volume appeared under the same editor in 2001 with the title *More What If?*

Historians have generally thought of such mind games as entertainments rather than serious intellectual endeavors. The subtitle of John Merriman's collection is *Chance and Humour in History,* while Robert Cowley opens his latest volume of speculations with the complaint that: "One of the troubles

This essay is an abridged version of Evans's Butterfield Lecture given at Queen's University, Belfast, in October 2002. It was published in the December 2002 issue of the *BBC History Magazine* and appeared in *Historically Speaking* 5 (March 2004) with the permission of the editors and author.

with history as it is studied today is that people take it too seriously." The earliest such collection, J. C. Squire's *If It Happened Otherwise: Lapses into Imaginary History,* treated the whole thing as a kind of whimsical parlor game (as Niall Ferguson has remarked, somewhat disapprovingly). Later collections, notably John Merriman's, do not seem to have escaped very far from such frivolity.

Yes, it's not just all good, clean, or in some cases not so clean fun. "History involving great people or pivotal events," complains Cowley, "is out of fashion. Broad trends, those waves that swell, break, and recede, are everything these days. We are left with the impression that history is inevitable, that what happened could not have happened any other way, and that drama and contingency have no place in the general scheme of human existence." The "what-if?" approach, he says, can help restore drama and contingency to the place that they ought rightfully to occupy. Cowley's complaint is, I think, unjustified: historical biography is as alive and flourishing as ever, microhistory has brought a new dimension of the personal and the particular into historical writing, and broad trends and ideas of historical inevitability are more out of fashion that in. Yes, in my admittedly rather old-fashioned view, there are broad general reasons for the proliferation of "what-if?" histories in recent years; the appearance of so many books advocating the return of chance and contingency to history is not just a matter of chance and contingency itself.

In the first place it's a reflection of the intellectual crisis and decline of Marxism, of modernization theory and social science–oriented history, and their replacement not just by postmodern playfulness but also by an emphasis on the arbitrariness of life as well as the text, if indeed it's possible to discern any difference between the two. There's a pervasive skepticism about the grand narratives in which historians have habitually scooped up facts and molded them into large, ordered patterns and a widespread rejection of any idea that history can ever be seen as moving in a particular direction determined by large-scale influences and irresistible forces. In sharing these views, "what-if?" collections are following a trend rather than bucking it.

Two contradictory steams of thoughts are at work here, I believe. The first is a degree of postmodern helplessness in the face of current events, as humanity seems to be drifting without direction, rudderless, in a post-ideological world, in which it no longer seems possible to believe in the idea of progress. This sense of disorientation is reflected in the kind of historical imagining that emphasizes the arbitrariness of human existence by claiming that tiny, chance events can have huge, uncontrollable consequences. Yes, emphasizing the importance of small events and individual human actions in history and downplaying the influence of large forces and broad trends could also be a way of restoring agency to human beings and reaffirming the possibility that we can all influence the course of history through our individual actions, no matter how ordinary we might be.

This perspective is linked in a good deal of speculative rewriting of the past to a view that it is not so much ordinary individuals like ourselves who alter history, as great men, great politicians, and in particular great generals. It's not by chance that Cowley's first collection was a set of essays on military history, or that so many "what-if?" essays focus on events like Hastings, Waterloo, the Armada, the Nazi invasion of the British Isles, and so on. This presupposes that not just battles but also, much more importantly, wars are won by generals alone and ignores the broader factors that most nonmilitary historians consider important, such as the economic strength, administrative efficiency, social cohesion, and logistical planning of the various combatant states. In a similar way, if speculative history is not about battles and generals, then it's often about kings and politicians. Yet few historians really believe that individuals operate on history without any external constraints. The choice is not between personalities and wider forces or circumstances; rather history involves in many cases the interaction of the two. To suppose that personal factors in great men, great generals, and great leaders are all that matter, even in military, diplomatic, and political history, is to indulge in oversimplification as drastic as that involved in saying they do not matter at all.

It's no accident, if I may use this well-worn cliché, that so many proponents of speculative history have been located on the right wing of the political spectrum. Niall Ferguson's collection on virtual history for example carries essays by such historians of the young fogey school as John Adamson, Jonathan Clark, Andrew Roberts, Michael Burleigh, and Mark Almond. Their arguments for chance and contingency in history are frequently directed against historians they regard as Marxist or at least socialist in orientation, such as E. H. Carr, Lawrence Stone, E. P. Thompson, or Eric Hobsbawm. In aiming at these historians they have a larger target in mind—the looming specter of determinism, which in Ferguson's view expresses the Marxist's "contempt for free will." Yet what's offered as a butt for criticism is often a caricature. Determinism simply means that historical events and processes are ultimately caused by factors independent of the individual human will. Contrary to what Ferguson claims, this does not mean that human will plays no part in history at all, nor did Marx and Engels ever say so. It does mean that people don't always get what they want.

Herbert Butterfield saw this elementary point clearly enough and put it forcefully in his most famous historiographical tract, *The Whig Interpretation of History*, published in 1931. Butterfield's principal concern in this book was to attack a history that looked at the past exclusively from the vantage point of the present and judged people in the past according to how much they had contributed to the state of the world at the time historian was writing. Yet in fact, he argued, what they actually wanted seldom really came to pass. The sixteenth-century Reformation, for instance, might be seen in retrospect as marking the beginning of the modern world. But it was not right, he said, to "take the Protestants of the sixteenth century as men who were fighting to bring about our modern world, while the Catholics were struggling to keep the medieval. Instead of seeing the modern world emerge as the victory of the children of light over the children of darkness in any generation, it is at least better to see it emerge as the result of a clash of wills, a result which often neither party wanted or even dreamed of, a result which indeed in some cases both parties would equally have hated."

Thus what happened in history, as least on the larger scale, was often not the result of human volition but could even run counter to it. Butterfield was not saying that human will and intentions played no part in history at all, merely that they seldom had a direct effect because one person's will and intentions seldom went unopposed by other people's. This idea is, surprisingly perhaps, very close to Marx and Engels's conception of the relationship between human will and historical change. As Engels wrote toward the end of his life, "History is made in such a way that the final result always arises from conflicts between many individual wills, of which each in turn has been made what it is by a host of particular conditions of life. Thus there are innumerable intersecting forces, an infinite series of parallelograms of forces which give rise to one resultant—the historical event."

Engels went on to insist, "We make our history ourselves, but under very definite assumptions and conditions." Marx put the essential point succinctly in his *Eighteenth Brumaire:* "People make their own history, but they do not make it just as they please; they do not make it under circumstances chosen by themselves, but under circumstances directly encountered, given, and transmitted from the past." Thus Marx and Engels always insisted, as they had to, on the need for revolutionary activism to take advantage of the circumstances in which the socialist movement found itself.

But while Marx and Engels gave due allowance to the operation of the human will, speculative history itself feeds off the very kind of large-scale, impersonal patterns and developments that it ostensibly tries to displace.

G. M. Trevelyan's counterfactual account of Napoleon's victory at Waterloo is actually a paean of praise to the English liberties he thought his real defeat had preserved; E. H. Carr's uncharacteristically free speculations on Lenin's survival into old age are actually an attempt to suggest that the horrors of Stalinism were not really the inevitable consequence of the Bolshevik Revolution. Nobody, on the other hand, would think it was worth asking what would have happened if the miller in Carlo Ginzburg's *Cheese and the Worms* had not held the strange beliefs that brought him before the Inquisition, just as nobody would think it worth speculating much on what might have been had the returning Martin Guerre in Natalie Zemon Davis's *Return of Martin Guerre* been the real Martin Guerre, or had Martin Guerre, real or false, not returned to his wife at all. There is no point in speculating on what might have happened unless the subject you are speculating on is a really big one in political, social, or economic terms and has thus been the object of historians' attempts to fit into big patterns of explanation.

Are such attempts inevitably determinist? Surely not. Most historical explanations implicitly admit that just one or two casual factors needed to be different for things to have turned out differently. If there hadn't been mass unemployment in Germany in the early 1930s, Hitler would not have come to power, for example. In this sense positing an alternative outcome can help weigh the influence or importance of the various factors we put together to build a casual explanation. Every real cause implies a counterfactual. This is important in trying to see how causes influence one another and come together to bring something about. But it's wrong to claim that we have to choose between believing that anything might have happened and thinking that everything was predetermined. In practice the search for causes, in history as in everyday life, concentrates on the areas between these two extremes.

So, too, in the end does Ferguson. Although he wants to restore an element of chance and contingency in history by looking at the possible alternatives to what happened, the number and variety of these possible alternatives are by no means infinite in his view; we have to confine ourselves to alternatives that are plausible, that is, courses of action or events that contemporaries actually considered. What happened was often not what contemporaries expected, so that the unrealized counterfactual scenario was the blueprint from which they were working when they took the decisions they did, and by studying this scenario we get a better idea why things turned out the way they did and why this was so often unexpected.

There is a problem in the requirement that only the alternatives actually consciously considered by contemporaries may be taken into account, because this implicitly confines the method to the history of politics and policies, diplomacy, war, and government, or, in other words, a very narrow area of history. Moreover, this requirement further restricts "what-if?" history to explanations of events. Yet history is not just about events, it's about many other things—processes, structures, cultures, societies, economies, and so on. Many major problems in history require explanations that are essentially impersonal, particularly in the areas of economic, social, and cultural history. What cotemporaries thought might have no relevance to what actually happened at all. Many people in the eighteenth and nineteenth centuries, for example, considered the possibility that the rural world might continue more or less unchanged, but that does not really help explain the Industrial Revolution.

It's one thing to examine the purposes and scenarios that existed in people's heads and quite another thing to extrapolate from these whole series of subsequent, never-realized long-term consequences that they quite clearly did not imagine. Ferguson argues, for example, that Britain's interests would not have been damaged by a German victory in a war from which the British stood aside: "A fresh assessment of Germany's pre-war aims reveal that, had Britain stood aside—even for a matter of weeks—continental Europe would have been transformed into something not unlike the European Union we know today—but without the massive contraction in British overseas power entailed by the fighting of two world wars."

Without British intervention, a German victory would have meant no German revolution in 1918, no Weimar Republic, no Hitler, no Holocaust, no Second World War. Britain's resources would have been untouched by the need to fight two major world wars and would have been enough to keep the British Empire going. The First World War was fought by the British, in other words, in an ultimately vain and hugely costly attempt to prevent what happened anyway—the creation of a German-dominated Europe. By fighting what Ferguson calls "Germany's first 'bid for European Union' . . . Asquith, Grey and their colleagues helped ensure that, when Germany did finally achieve predominance on the continent, Britain was no longer strong enough to provide a check to it."

Now none of this speculation in my view helps explain why the British Cabinet decided to go to war in August 1914. It is surely enough to know that the cabinet feared the consequences of a German victory in a continental war; we don't really need to know whether or not they were right to do so. A similar line is taken by other right-wing historians who argue that if Britain had made a separate peace with Germany in 1940, then the British overseas empire would not have been lost, and Britain would have remained a world power, to the benefit of all. These arguments, I believe, are wrong in several respects. First, it is a grotesque and absurd oversimplification to describe the European Union today as a vehicle for the German domination of Europe. The European Union is simply too large and complex an entity to sustain sweeping, politically motivated generalizations of this kind. Even describing it slightly more accurately as resting on the joint hegemony of Germany and France ignores the way in which key decisions have to be taken through the council of ministries, with a single-country veto on crucial issues. If we look at the European Commission or the European Parliament, we do not see German domination here, rather the reverse, with particularly strong weight given to the smaller countries. Nor does European legislation amount to an export of German law into other countries. In the end the caricature of the European Union as a new German Empire, even a Fourth Reich, as graphically illustrated in an anti-Euro advertisement screened in British cinemas in the summer of 2003, with the comedian Rik Mayall dressed as Hitler screaming his approval of *"Ein Volk, Ein Reich, Ein Euro,"* is a convenient piece of propaganda designed to link the fight against the euro with the potent collective memory of Britain standing alone against a German-dominated Europe in 1940. In fact, of course, the European Union was created by Hitler's opponents and embodies values that Hitler hated; and it's not surprising that Rik Mayall's antics drew criticism when the advertisement was screened.

There is plenty of evidence that Germany's longer-term foreign-policy aims leading up to both 1914 and 1939 went much further than merely establishing economic hegemony over the European continent. In both cases there are clear contemporary indications that the German government was issuing a challenge among other things to British world power. Nobody can prove that Britain would have kept the Empire had it remained neutral in 1939–45; on the other hand, there is a huge amount of evidence to indicate that the continued rise of American power, on the one hand, and more importantly the changing and evolving nature of society and politics in the Indian, African, and other colonies, on the other, were the real forces behind decolonization in the post–Second World War era. In other words this was a process no amount of money and resources saved by the Britain not spending billions on pounds on the war effort could have brought to a halt.

Much of the allegedly counterfactual history of the New Right is in the end little more than a rather obvious form of wishful thing. "What if" is really little more than "if only"; and in this form it contributes nothing to our understanding of what actually did happen, because its concern is not really with examining how and why people like Grey or Churchill took the decisions they took but rather with pointing out supposedly preferable alternatives and bemoaning the fact that they never came to pass. Speculative history comes in two guises: the liberal, whiggish guise, adopted for example by G. M. Trevelyan, where it's designed to show how much worse were the possible alternatives to what happened; and the conservative, pessimistic guise, adopted for example by Niall Ferguson, where it's designed to show how much better.

Far from liberating history from an imaginary straitjacket of Marxist determinism, alternative, speculative histories confine it in another that is far more constricting. This is because the counterfactual in the sense of an alternative future—in the sense of "what if A had happened instead of B?"—assumes or posits a whole series of other things that would have inevitably followed: "If A had happened instead of B, then inevitably, C, D, and E would have inevitably followed instead of what actually happened, namely, X, Y, and Z." But of course a thousand other things might or would have intervened to make this alternative course of events completely unpredictable.

As Jonathan Clark notes in his own contribution to *Virtual History,* "The contingent and counterfactual are only congruent at the outset of any historical enquiry. Soon, they begin to pull in different directions. The counterfactual assumes clearly identifiable alternative paths of development, whose distinctness and coherence can be relied on as the historian projects them into an unrealized future. An emphasis on contingency, by contrast, not only contends that the way in which events unfold followed no such path . . . it also entails that all counterfactual alternatives would themselves have quickly branched out into an infinite number of possibilities."

In other words, the deployment of the "what-if?" type of argument to posit a long-term alternative development assumes (a) the absence of any further contingencies and chances along the way and (b) the absolute predictability of all possible ways in which the initial alternative event influenced, or did not influence, subsequent history. All of this removes chance and contingency from history almost totally. Instead of restoring open futures to the past, it closes them off.

Altering one part of the kaleidoscope of history shakes up all the others in ways that are so unpredictable as to make either medium- or long-term alternative scenarios completely unconvincing. History in the end is and can only really be about finding out what happened and what was and understanding and explaining it, not positing alternative courses of development or indulging in bouts of wishful thinking about what might have been.

Is the Dark Light Enough?

Edward Ingram

How one envies Richard J. Evans his certainties, his Manichaean view of the world. For him, what happened is good: it happened. What did not happen is bad; not bad in itself, merely a quicksand wise historians will not tread in. And to be so certain that one knows what happened that one also knows what did not; that one can tell the one from the other. The difficulty facing the rest of us unfortunates in appraising the worth of counterfactuals lies not in working out what did *not* happen but what *did*.

Less-obvious sleight of hand will be needed if Evans is to find a part-time job as a conjuror. What pretends to be a discussion of counterfactuals is nothing of the kind; neither theory nor method receives much of a mention. Evans ignores Philip E. Tetlock's work on the control of counterfactuals, even though few historians would challenge three of its basic propositions: that one can avoid counterfactuals only by forgoing causal inference, that counterfactuals help to minimize the extent to which hindsight closes off lines of inquiry, and that the principle of the minimal rewrite should govern their use.[1]

Evans merely uses one counterfactual proposition about Great Britain's role in the two world wars as a weapon with which to attack a school of historians whom he calls "young fogeys." One of their faults, apparently, is a preference for event and individual to structure and process, for contingency to determinism. He rebukes them for believing in "butterfly effects": one classic illustration of chaos theory postulates that the chance beating of the wings of a butterfly up the Amazon River may result in a hurricane ravaging Bermuda. But chaos theory is determinist. Or so E. H. Carr thought. The car crash he uses as a metaphor for causation in *What Is History?* could easily have been determined by the wings of a butterfly that happened, while beating, to catch the eye of one of his drivers. Nobody would mistake Carr for a "young fogey," despite the pleasure he took in prolonging Lenin's life.

The apparently sitting ducks at which Evans takes potshots peck him on the nose. How can it help us, he states, to ask what if Napoleon had won the battle of Waterloo? Here is one answer: it would have prevented Englishmen who write patriotic history in the style of Arthur Bryant from claiming that the Duke of Wellington won. Victory is not the clear-cut phenomenon Evans implies. Nor is any other type of event. The past happened. But what happened, we do not know and cannot find out. We can only try to represent what *may* have happened. Thus the historian's rule: the more apparently incontrovertible the statement about the more apparently undeniable the event, the less one is likely to learn from it. The obvious example is the Holocaust. It happened. One may not say that it did not. But what does that tell us about it? To find out when, why, to whom, at what speed, and in what circumstances it happened, one has to state a series of counterfactual propositions. The best way to learn more about the past is by asking: what if something else?

Evans pretends that for him, unlike the "young fogeys," events do not matter. Or they matter less than structure and process, which cannot be counterfactualized. But they can, and they must, because often they turn out to be chimeras luring devotees of the *longue durée* into the desert. The Industrial Revolution used to be the most celebrated process in British history. It *happened,* and in the 125 years from the mid-eighteenth to the mid-nineteenth century, it transformed Britain's political and economic systems, social structure, and culture. But why may we not have asked, what if it had *not* happened, when now we are told that it didn't? It may have begun in Britain (although continental Europeans have their doubts), but as it was never finished, it changed little. A relay race in which the baton of industrialization was passed early from Britain to the Continent to the United States, left Britain on the sidelines, anchored in the *ancien régime.* Today's nineteenth-century Britain would have been unrecognizable fifty years ago.

When working out what happened, Evans recommends reliance on common sense applied to established facts. As we establish more facts, our account becomes more reliable. But facts have no existence independent of us, or, if they have (in the sense that events and processes did happen, whether we know of them or not), we may not recognize them even after we have stubbed our toes bumping into them. Without working through the series of possible explanations suggested by counterfactuals, we have little chance, when peering into the fogbound North Atlantic, of telling the iceberg from the *Titanic*. Take the subject of one of Evans's most severe criticisms of the "young fogeys": Britain's decision to go to war in 1914. For Evans the explanation of the decision is simple and established: the British elite feared the results of a German victory. That is all we need to know, given that he confines our task when explaining events to entering into the minds of the dead.

One is surprised to find someone who proclaims an interest in structure and process so easily satisfied. What if the British did not go to war in 1914 but merely declared war? What if they were worried about Russia rather than Germany? Or were bandwagoning rather than balancing? Or were thinking about the wider world rather than the Continent? Why does nothing change? That the reasons for Britain's decision to go war in 1914 have been around for so long should give any structuralist cause to question them. The Germans changed their paradigm forty years ago when Fritz Fischer revealed the extent of Germany's war aims. The English, who nodded in agreement—they already knew—now ignore Paul W. Schroeder's claim that one may not attribute the outbreak of war to the Central Powers' actions alone. The destabilizing of the international system resulted partly from Britain's treatment of Austria-Hungary.

To understand what happened in the past, one must face the right way, looking forward into the future, not backward like Evans. The events of 1914 are contentious because they illustrate the most common use of a particular type of counterfactual. They form part of a series that runs backward, against the clock and the calendar, in which later events cause earlier ones and, by so doing, alter, in this case, the process by which general peace turns into general war. By changing the causes of the First World War, one changes the working of the Bismarckian system, which in its turn changes the results and causes of the Crimean War. Grey and Bethmann-Hollweg determine the actions of Palmerston and Napoleon III.

The events of 1914 lie in the middle not at the beginning of the sequence. The emphasis on Germany in 1914 derives from the self-congratulation of Englishmen on their exemplary behavior during their supposedly finest hour, when they alone stood up to Hitler. That they destroyed Great Britain as a result was a price, Evans implies, worth paying. For he allows himself to say that the choice was right while not allowing the "young fogeys" to say that it was wrong. And despite his rejection of counterfactuals, he relies on one to rebut their claim that Great Britain's self-destruction was unnecessary: in his opinion, postwar anticolonialism and the rise of the United States would have destroyed it anyway. A false conclusion: the events of the early cold war prove the readiness of the Truman administration to buttress any colonialist regime that could pass itself off as anticommunist. A false prediction: Robert Jervis shows that one may not change one characteristic of a system while implying that the others will continue to operate as they had. And false historical reasoning: one cannot find out why the British took such rash, and foolish, decisions without asking what might have been the results of the choices they rejected.

Evans, who objects to the use of the term *foolish*, as well as to the use of counterfactuals, misreads the minds he tells us to enter. Jock Colville's description of the bloated Winston Churchill quaffing at Ditchley the vintage champagne he sponged off his American millionaire host, Ronald Tree, leaves one wondering whether, for him, the war had much to do with fighting either Nazis or greater Germany. Churchill relished the excitement and the high life, the applause not the cause. And why, as Noel Coward asks, must the show go on? Other national heroes, Havelock of Lucknow and Lawrence of Arabia, take their solos in the spotlight, then retire, often no longer noticed, to the wings. If they are fortunate, in time they are given another turn. But Churchill never leaves the stage. Perhaps for Englishmen of the age of Margaret Thatcher, who said that Britain had not won the Second World War in order that Germany should be reunited, the war never ends. But why should it provide the imaginative and emotional foundation for the lives of their children?

The obsession with Nazism and the glorification of Britain's role in the Second World War is attributable partly to Churchill's success in peddling the self-portrait he painted in his memoirs of the savior of the nation. It is also partly attributable to the influence of the distinguished Central European émigrés who have held senior positions in the British academy. They look at British history from a peculiar standpoint. To them, an interest in continental politics appears natural, as well as desirable, to an extent that would have surprised earlier generations of Englishmen. A colleague said in 1798 of Lord Grenville, the foreign secretary who collected maps, that he knew nothing of events beyond the Rhine. Seven years earlier the political elite had forced William Pitt the Younger to dismiss Grenville's predecessor for arguing that Britain had the capability—and ought to try—to control political change in Central and Eastern Europe. Catherine II of Russia soon showed him his mistake.

If one looks forward from the nineteenth century instead of backward from the mid-twentieth, one hears in the discussions about whether to go to war in 1914 and to go on fighting in 1940, the echoes of similar discussions in 1870, 1853, and notably 1800, the moment when the British did decide, in the middle of a world war, to make a truce after they had stabilized their strategic position. They chose, sensibly, not to go on fighting, in a bid to limit the economic dislocation and social unrest. They applied the rule again, successfully in 1853 and unsuccessfully in 1914, that someone else could be found, more interested, on the same side and willing to take the lead and pay the price. They waited for Austria and Russia to destroy Napoleon on their behalf; offering to pay some of the bills but taking care, while being on the winning side, not to fight in the crucial battles. Waterloo was not one of them.

Despite Evans's interest in process and structure, his treatment of Britain's role in the world wars privileges intention over action. What men do matters more than why they do it. When political scientists see actors taking, over time, a series of identical or similar actions (measured against a predetermined theoretical rule), they ignore the variety of reasons that may have prompted the behavior. The British were trying in the First World War to replay the game they had played against Napoleon and later Nicholas I rather than practicing for the game they would play against Hitler.

The Industrial Revolution happened or did not happen, whether or not Jane Austen and Walter Scott were aware of it. Evans's idealist approach to events leaves too much unanswered because unasked. Readers of histories want to know not only what contemporaries *thought* was happening but also what *was*. Evans doubtless approves of military historians who, in recounting the events of a battle, refuse to disclose what was happening beyond the brow of the hill. Both commanders, wreathed in smoke, their gallopers killed or their radios defunct, may not have known why one lost and the other won. Historians have to try to find out.

For anyone interested in process and structure, a historical explanation is the application of a theory. To test it, one applies it to a series of cases held to be similar and to test their similarity applies counterfactuals. Collecting more evidence and establishing its validity do not help. If political science teaches nothing else, it demonstrates the inability of evidence to invalidate theory. Far from decrying the use of counterfactuals, we should make them compulsory: without practice in using them, we fail to recognize the assumptions underlying our questionable statements. And we should question them daily.

Historical explanations, even of the role of Great Britain in 1914 and 1940, do not aspire to the status of laws written by Medes and Persians.

NOTE

1. See, for example, Philip E. Tetlock and Aaron Belkin, eds., *Counterfactual Thought Experiments in World Politics: Logical, Methodological, and Psychological Perspectives* (Princeton, N.J.: Princeton University Press, 1996), chap. 1.

Good History Needs Counterfactuals

Richard Ned Lebow

R ichard Evans is right on target in his criticism of Niall Ferguson's simplistic and ideologically transparent use of counterfactuals. Ferguson's two books do a disservice to counterfactuals, which remain an essential—if inadequately exploited—tool of historical and social scientific research.

Robert Cowley's two volumes, by contrast, make no pretense about using counterfactuals to do anything other than to alert readers to just how contingent the past really was. This is a useful exercise because the "hindsight bias" (one of the more robust and most heavily documented cognitive biases) leads us to overvalue the likelihood of events that have already occurred. Historical research reinforces this bias. R. H. Tawney observed that it gives "an appearance of inevitableness" to an existing order by dragging into prominence the forces that have triumphed and thrusting into the background those that were swallowed up.[1] No matter how well documented or convincingly presented, historical studies invariably provoke critiques and contending interpretations. Decades—or centuries—of controversy about such events as the French Revolution or the fall of the Roman Empire generate shelves of studies that attribute these developments to a wide range of political, economic, social, and intellectual causes. Discount a half-dozen putative causes, and another half-dozen still remain. Historical debate encourages the belief that events like the rise of the West, the Industrial Revolution, World War I, and the end of the Cold War were massively "overdetermined."

A counterfactual is a "what if" statement about the past. By mutating a feature of the past (such as, Hitler is killed on the Western Front in World War I), we make a case for the present being in some way different (such as, there

From *Historically Speaking* 5 (March 2004)

was no Holocaust). The plausibility of any such claim depends on the feasibility of the antecedent (the odds were heavily against a frontline soldier surviving as long as Hitler did) and the chain of historical logic linking it to the proposed consequent. As Henry Turner has argued, it seems likely that some form of conservative, revanchist regime would have come to power in Germany in the 1930s and would probably have gone to war against Poland to regain lost territory. But without Hitler, there would have been no war of extermination against the Jews. Good counterfactuals—and one of the many reasons why Ferguson's mutations of history do not qualify—must also consider what else might have happened as a result of the antecedent and the implications of these developments for the consequent. Ferguson contends that General Ludendorff's 1913 plan for adding 300,000 men to the German army was financially and politically feasible (doubtful) and would have made Germany more inclined toward peace (more dubious still) and would have provided the extra manpower to make the Schlieffen Plan work. He fails entirely to consider how France and Russia might have reacted. If each country had increased its conscription by only half as much, the German General Staff would have been right back where it started.

Counterfactuals are critical to good history. They are fundamental to all causal statements. If we claim that x caused y, we assume y would not have happened—*ceteris paribus*—in the absence of x. Quantitative research attempts to get around this problem by constructing a sample of comparable cases large enough to contain adequate variation on dependent and independent variables. Historians typically attempt to establish causation by process tracing. They try to document the links between a stated cause and a given outcome, a strategy particularly appropriate to the individual level of analysis when there is enough evidence to document the calculations and motives of actors. Even when such evidence is available, it may still not be possible to determine the relative weight of the several hypothesized causes and which, if any, might have produced the outcome in the absence of others or in combination with other causes not at work in the case. To sustain causal inference it is necessary to engage in comparative analysis to explore what would have happened in the absence of x. Within the single-case format, comparative analysis can take the form of intracase or counterfactual analysis.

Intracase comparison breaks down a case into a series of similar interactions that are treated as separate and independent cases for purposes of analysis. The goal is to generate as much variation as possible on dependent (*explanandum*) and independent (the *explanans*) variables. This is sometimes more difficult to do than in cross-case comparisons. The independence of cases is also more problematic, as the process and outcome of past decisions are likely to have considerable influence on subsequent decisions about similar issues. But intracase comparison confers a singular benefit: it builds variation within a fundamentally similar political and cultural context, controlling better than intercase comparison for many factors that may be important but otherwise unrecognized.

When intracase comparison is impossible, variation can only be generated within a case by counterfactual experimentation. This latter strategy lies at the core of many scientific simulations where variables are given a wide range of counterfactual values to determine the sensitivity of the outcome to changes in one or more of them. Counterfactual simulation can identify key variables and the range of values in which they will have the most impact on the outcome. Information obtained this way, especially if it has counterintuitive implications, can guide subsequent empirical work intended to generate information necessary to better represent reality.

Counterfactual speculation can tease out the assumptions—often unarticulated—on which historical interpretations rest. Many students of the Soviet Union contend that Stalin, or somebody like him, was the unavoidable product of a political system based on central rule and terror. Apologists for communism like E. H. Carr insist that the Soviet Union would have evolved differently if Lenin had lived longer or had been succeeded by someone other than Stalin. Attempts to address this question have compelled historians to be more explicit about the underlying assumptions that guide and sustain contending interpretations of Stalin and the nature of the Communist party and the Soviet state. Those assumptions have now become the focus of controversy, and scholars have looked for empirical evidence with which to evaluate them. This process has encouraged a more sophisticated historical debate.

Counterfactuals are an essential part of evaluation. Was the development of nuclear weapons a blessing or a curse for humankind? What about affirmative action, free trade, or the growing economic and political integration of Europe? Serious and thoughtful scholars can be found on all sides of these controversies. Their arguments share one thing in common: they use counterfactual benchmarks—most often, implicitly—to assess the merits of real-world policies, outcomes, or trends. Proponents of nuclear weapons who claim that nuclear weapons had beneficial consequences during the cold war imagine a superpower war, or at least a higher probability of one, in the absence of nuclear deterrence. Some critics of nuclear weapons, like John Mueller, argue that self-deterrence, based on memories of the horrors of conventional war, would have kept the peace. Others contend that they sustained the cold war, and that it would have been less intense, and possibly resolved earlier, in the absence of nuclear weapons.

Assessment can be significantly influenced, or even determined, by the choice of counterfactual. The conventional wisdom holds that the Allied victory in World War I was a good thing: it prevented an expansionist, continental power from achieving hegemony in continental Europe. This assessment represents the view of the world from the corporate boardrooms and corridors of power in London, New York, and Washington. From the perspective of say, Polish Jewry, the outcome was a disaster. If Germany had won, it is highly unlikely that there would have been a Hitler or a Holocaust. In this case the choice of counterfactual reflects the different interests of the groups. As with historical analogies, the interesting question is the extent to which counterfactuals guide evaluation or are chosen to justify positions that people have reached for quite different reasons.

Counterfactuals are routinely relied on by policymakers to make critical decisions. One of the principal policy "lessons" of the 1930s was that appeasement whets the appetites of dictators while military capability and resolve restrains them. The failure of Anglo-French efforts to appease Hitler is well established, but the putative efficacy of deterrence rests on the counterfactual that Hitler *could* have been restrained *if* France and Britain had demonstrated willingness to go to war in defense of the European territorial status quo. German documents make this an eminently researchable question, and historians have used these documents to try to determine at what point Hitler could no longer be deterred. The Kennedy administration based its policy in the Cuban missile crisis on the assumption—that we now know to have been false—that Khrushchev would not have sent missiles to Cuba if they had practiced deterrence more firmly. The president and his advisors accordingly felt the need to risk war to demonstrate resolve to prevent a follow-up move by Khrushchev against Berlin. Soviet documents and interviews with former leaders and advisors indicate that Khrushchev sent missiles to Cuba because he felt the need to deter Kennedy, whom he considered young and reckless, from invading Cuba and exploiting American strategic superiority to bully the Soviet Union.[2]

The study of why and how people use counterfactuals to work their way through problems is essential to understanding personal and policy decisions. The validity of these counterfactuals will have important implications for our assessment of these decisions, just as the validity (or lack of it) of the deterrence counterfactual provides a necessary baseline for our evaluation of French and British policy in the 1930s, American national security policy during the cold war, and contemporary applications of the strategy of deterrence.

Historians often dismiss counterfactuals as "parlor games" because they allegedly rest on speculation, not fact. The deterrence counterfactuals were subject to the same kind of empirical validation as any other historical argument once the relevant documents became available. Some historical counterfactuals even lend themselves to quantitative testing. Jay M. Winter exploited counterfactual projections of mortality rates based on prewar data from Prudential Life Insurance policies to determine the age structure of British war losses. He combined data from the life tables for 1913 and 1915 in roughly two-to-one proportions, as the war did not begin until August 1914, to create a counterfactual table for 1914. On the basis of the prior decade, he calculated what the life tables would have been for the period 1914–18 in the absence of war. By comparing the actual death rates in each age group with the counterfactual estimates, he was able to determine the death rates of five-year cohorts for each year of the war and to show that the British government consistently lied about the extent of its war losses.[3]

When evidence is meager or absent, the difference between counterfactual and "factual" history may still be marginal. Documents are rarely "smoking guns" that allow researchers to establish motives or causes beyond a reasonable doubt. Actors only occasionally leave evidence about their motives, and historians rarely accept such testimony at face value. More often, historians infer motives from what they know about actors: personalities and goals, their past behavior, and the constraints under which they operated. In his highly acclaimed study of the Peloponnesian War, Donald Kagan argues that Pericles wanted to ally with Corcyra in the expectation that it would deter Sparta from going to the aid of Corinth. If deterrence failed, Athens, protected by its city walls and the long walls to its harbor at Piraeus, would refuse to engage the main body of Spartan forces even if they invaded Attica and laid waste to its olive orchards and vineyards. After a few years of frustration, Pericles expected the Spartans to recognize the futility of waging war against Athens. He also expected the peace faction, led by King Archidamus, to regain power, and the two hegemons to reach a more lasting accommodation. This scenario is purely speculative and intended to explain away behavior that would otherwise appear unenlightened and warlike.[4]

When we move from individual actors to small groups, elites, societies, states, and regional and international systems, the balance between evidence and inference shifts decisively in the direction of the latter. Structural arguments assume that behavior is a response to the constraints and opportunities generated by a set of domestic or international conditions. Mark Elvin's elegant study of China starts from the premise that empires expand to the point at which their technological superiority over their neighbors is approximately counterbalanced by the burdens of size. At this equilibrium, imperial social institutions come under constant strain because of the high relative cost of security. Harsh taxation impoverishes peasant cultivators and leads to falling tax revenues. The ensuing decline in the number of free subjects makes military recruitment more difficult, and governments rely instead on barbarian auxiliaries, even for their main fighting forces. To save money, governments also give up active defense policies and try to keep hostile barbarians at bay through diplomacy, bribery, and settlement on imperial lands. The inevitable outcome is a weakened economic base, barbarization from within, and, finally, partial or total collapse of the empire. Elvin musters considerable evidence in support of his thesis, much of it from primary sources, but it is all in the way of illustration. Nowhere is he able to show that Chinese leaders pursued any of the policies he describes for any of the reasons he attributes to them.[5]

For the most part then, structural arguments are built on a chain of inference that uses behavioral principles as anchor points. Empirical evidence, when available, may be exploited to suggest links between these principles and behavior. But even in the best of cases these links are indirect and presumptive and can be corroborated only obliquely and incompletely. Readers evaluate these arguments on the seeming "reasonableness" of the inferences made, the quality and relevance of the evidence offered in support, and the extent to which that evidence permits or constrains alternative interpretations. Receptivity to arguments is significantly influenced by the appeal of the underlying political and behavioral principles in which the inferences are rooted. When these principles run counter to the reigning orthodoxy, the arguments may be dismissed out of hand regardless of the evidence.

Good counterfactual thought experiments differ little from "factual" modes of historical reconstruction. If we attempt to evaluate the importance of Mikhail Gorbachev for the end of the cold war by considering the likely consequences of Chernenko being succeeded by someone else, we need to study the career and policies of other possible successors (such as, Grishin, Romanov, Ligachev) and infer their policies on the basis of their past preferences and commitments, the political environment in 1985, and the general domestic and foreign situation of the Soviet Union. There is a lot of evidence about all three questions, evidence that sustains informed arguments about the kind of domestic and foreign policies these leaders might have pursued. Admittedly, unexpected events, like Mathias Rust's Cessna flight to Red

Square in May 1987, which Gorbachev exploited to purge the military of many hardliners, can also have significant influence on policy.

Counterfactual arguments are only as compelling as the logic and "evidence" offered to substantiate the links between the hypothesized antecedent and its expected consequences. Every good counterfactual rests on multiple "factuals," just as every factual rests on counterfactual assumptions, and these linkages need to be addressed by historians. Social "facts," moreover, are reflections of the concepts we use to describe social reality, not of reality itself. They are ideational and subjective, and even the existence of "precise" measures for them—something we only rarely have—would not make them any less arbitrary. For, as the philosopher Willard V. O. Quine has shown, theoretical concepts insinuate themselves into the "data language" of even the hardest sciences. The construction of "factual" history is therefore entirely imaginary, and its only claim to privilege is that the concepts and categories in terms of which it is constructed tell us something useful or interesting about the social world. The same holds true for counterfactual history.

NOTES

1. R. H. Tawney, *The Agrarian Problem in the Sixteenth Century* (London: Longmans, Green, 1912), 177.

2. Richard Ned Lebow and Janice Gross Stein, *We All Lost the Cold War* (Princeton, N.J.: Princeton University Press, 1994), chap. 2.

3. Jay M. Winter, *The Great War and the British People* (New York: Macmillan, 1986), 76–83.

4. Donald Kagan, *The Outbreak of the Peloponnesian War* (Ithaca, N.Y.: Cornell University Press, 1969), 203–342.

5. Mark Elvin, *The Pattern of the Chinese Past: A Social and Economic Interpretation* (Palo Alto, Calif.: Stanford University Press, 1973).

Counterfactuals and the Historical Imagination

William H. McNeill

Historians can playfully ask, "What if?" and historians can be foolish when writing imaginary history, too. But there is a serious intellectual kernel behind the game, for there are events, like the failure of the siege of Jerusalem in 701 B.C.E., that did make a quite extraordinary difference in what followed. And by drawing attention to such occasions and wondering out loud how different the world would be, contingent, surprising, unpredictable aspects of the human past can become obvious to most readers. This seems worthwhile to me, since oversimplified schemes for explaining human affairs abound, and we are continually tempted to believe everything was somehow always inevitable.

Evans's arguments against counterfactual history seem rather trivial to me. Too often he sets up straw men to demolish. Surely no one supposes that "individuals operate on history without any external constraints"; and I don't believe anyone thinks that "only the alternatives actually considered by contemporaries may be taken into account." Which is not to say that counterfactual historians do not sometimes rewrite history in silly and misleading ways, as Evans says they do.

But suitably restrained reflection on the consequences of particular events opens our eyes to contingency and can sharpen awareness of the role of human agency in the historical process we would like to understand and, as historians, persistently try to describe and anatomize, knowing all the while how inadequate our words and concepts are for the job we set ourselves.

The fact is that human beings have always lived within an evolving system of enormous complexity where uncertainty prevails. This is true of the

From *Historically Speaking* 5 (March 2004)

entire universe from the Big Bang until the present; it is true of Earth's ecosystem within which we exist; and it is true of human societies of every size and shape and of interactions across time. The whole constitutes a web of interconnectedness, interdependence, and emerging complexities whose future is as unpredictable as was each transformation of its truly surprising past.

Within that web, humans occupy a peculiar place on Earth and perhaps even in the universe. For after our ancestors became fully human by learning to speak and then began to act together on the basis of agreed-upon meanings, they introduced a new level of disturbance into the world around them. Our history swiftly became a truly amazing story of how humankind enlarged its ecological niche at the expense of other life-forms by diverting more and more energy flows to suit our own particular wishes.

As a result, human consciousness, plans, and concerted actions turned out to have profoundly disturbing consequences for ourselves and for Earth's other life forms. We even affect climate and the chemical and physical equilibria of air, sea, and soil. To be sure, humans seldom or never got exactly what they hoped for. Unexpected side effects and outright disappointments prevail, only to provoke new actions, new forms of behavior, and, over time, new ways of getting what we want. Human actions consequently became the most active variable affecting biological evolution; and all this started several hundred thousand years ago when our ancestors learned to control fire and began to burn landscapes deliberately.

Among ourselves, conscious purposes and plans weave a web of competition and cooperation so complex that no one fully comprehends it. This is where historians mostly concentrate their attention, and not without reason since large-scale upshots, manifest in the actions of states, armies, and other powerful human groups, matter for everyone and everything around them. That is because, being powerful, they are able to intrude upon, alter, and crush opposition far and near, at home and abroad, and today literally around the Earth as shown by recent events in Iraq.

Yet such power does not assure expected results. Surprises, often unwelcome, continue to arise—not least in Iraq. Nonetheless, we historians are professionally committed to explaining what happens, thus making the human world around us more nearly understandable and perhaps channelling future collective behavior along lines more likely to escape disaster and minimize unwelcome surprises.

The task is beyond human power today and probably always will be. But not to try our very best to understand what happens around us is an abdication of a perennial human aspiration. Once it was shamans who interrogated the spirits in hope of finding answers. Later priests and prophets invoked a multiplicity of gods; then used sacred scriptures to decipher God's will. More recently, scientists and historians came along, inventing notions about processes and patterns that, perhaps, might explain what happened. But an accurate history of the past and precise forecasting of the future were never definitively attained either for the natural world around us or for human society itself. Not even the stars are fixed forever in their courses, as recent theories and observations make clear. And despite our best efforts to make our behavior more nearly predictable through customs, laws, and religious commandments, human societies remained volatile—ever so powerful, ever so complicated, and stubbornly unpredictable. Yet because human hopes and purposes so often met disappointment, historians remained on the whole more modest in trying to explain what happened than physicists and astronomers once were.

Now, however, physicists and astronomers have joined us in recognizing an evolving universe where surprises prevail. All the sciences and all the religions of the Earth are alike in seeking to understand and give meaning to the grand process within which we exist. All fall short of definitive success. So we live as always with uncertainty about past and future; and all of us persist in trying to understand, in his or her own way, what to believe, what to do, and what to say about who and what we are and how we got here.

Agreement on these matters is a matter of faith and not of sure and certain knowledge. But agreement is nonetheless an important, even an essential, support for common action. Shaping some sort of loose consensus among a part of humankind is as much as practicing historians, scientists, theologians, politicians, journalists, and other professional soothsayers can expect in any foreseeable future. If the learned professions and politicians cooperate, interrogate one another, and consider the courses of events and weigh the data each sort of specialist assembles and argues about, then local clusters of workable hypotheses and agreed-upon ideas may continue, as they have in the past, to guide collective human actions and raise some populations to positions of power over others who find it harder to agree.

That, at least, is what historians and their fellow intellectuals have done before and will, I suppose, continue to do in time to come. Assuredly the job of constructing credible ideas about the past and trying to make human affairs intelligible is a high and serious calling. We share and compete with other professions in defining such ideas. Discussion of what did not happen can be a useful part of that effort, sobering and often amusing as well. Let us therefore continue to exercise the far reaches of historical imagination and cheerfully ask, "What if?" from time to time.

The New Counterfactualists

Allan Megill

To make sense of so-called counterfactual history, we need to get clear about the theoretical issues that counterfactuality raises. We also need to make some distinctions. I would begin with a distinction between two types of counterfactual history, "restrained" and "exuberant." Restrained counterfactual history involves an explicit canvassing of alternative possibilities that existed in a real past, whereas exuberant counterfactual history deals in past historical outcomes that never in fact came to be.

Exuberant counterfactual history diverges radically from normal historical research and writing. This is the kind of counterfactual history that tries to imagine what might have resulted if Britain had intervened in the American Civil War, if an Irish Home Rule Bill had passed the British parliament in 1912, or if Germany had invaded Britain in 1940. All three of these imagined situations appear in Niall Ferguson's edited volume *Virtual History.*[1] This sort of counterfactual history is indeed better called "virtual history," to emphasize that it addresses no *actual* past—or "imaginary history," to emphasize its lack of groundedness. Virtual history evokes "virtual reality." It also evokes the world of historically based game playing: one thinks, for example, of the well-known board game *Axis and Allies,* now available in a computer version, which attempts to simulate World War II from 1942 onward.[2] Such games allow players to go back to some chosen point in historical time and make decisions that diverge from the decisions made by the real historical actors. What then eventuates results from chance and also (this is no small matter) from assumptions embedded in the game by its makers. There is no pretension here

Revised from *Historically Speaking* 5 (March 2004)

to be replaying historical reality, at least none that a grown-up could take seriously. It is a *game,* dressed up with certain features of a real past.

When professional historians write virtual history, we ought to treat their claims concerning "what might have been" with about the same distanced skepticism with which we would treat the playing out of World War II by a group of fifteen-year-olds. One can certainly speak of plausibilities, but the plausibilities are far harder to judge than *normal* historical plausibilities, which are tied down to a world that actually existed. When historians imagine what might have happened if John F. Kennedy had not been shot or if the USSR had avoided collapse, they are on shaky epistemological ground. Historians must always speculate, but speculations concerning virtual history are far more deeply permeated by undersupported assumptions about the real nature of the world than is the case when the normal canons of historical method operate. Indeed, quite apart from the specific ideological preferences of the historian or game-maker, virtual history cannot be invented nor the game played without a set of rules that are in large measure arbitrary. These assumptions constitute a "theory" about how the world normally operates that may or may not be true. To make inferences on the basis of such assumptions is to engage in a "top-down" inferential reasoning that is epistemologically much more problematic than "bottom-up" inference.

It will clarify matters if we look at virtual history in the light of issues of temporality. The virtual historian cuts into the real past at some particular moment—normally just before one of the historical actors involved made a weighty decision. The virtual historian conceptualizes this moment as one of contingency, in which the decision *could* have been rendered differently and in which, subsequently, matters *might* have gone in a particular other direction. The virtual historian exploits the supposed contingency at the beginning in order to launch his or her counterfactual history. But contingency cuts two ways. Contingency and the freedom entailed by the very idea of a human capacity to decide give virtual history its opening. But the same contingency that makes virtual history possible also undermines it. If we have contingency in its beginning, we must surely have contingency in its early middle: to paraphrase Weber, contingency is not a train one can get on or off at will. This means that virtual history cannot follow any definable course at all. More precisely, it can follow a definable course only until the next contingency arises. Although the virtual historian may well try to get away with claiming a normal historian's authority, once past this moment of renewed contingency he is better thought of as a writer of imaginative literature. This is not necessarily bad, but it is not history.

Virtual history ought not to be confused with counterfactual history in general. Virtual history starts out from a moment in the real past where things might have worked out differently and then moves *forward* in time, getting ever further from a world that existed. "Restrained" counterfactual history moves from observed effect to hypothesized causes. It starts out from an actual event, such as the English Civil War, and then looks back in time, canvassing how it might have come to pass that the Civil War might *not* have occurred (or might have occurred in a sharply different way). In Ferguson's anthology, John Adamson's essay "England without Cromwell: What If Charles I Had Avoided the Civil War?" is in large measure an exercise of this sort. Adamson canvasses a variety of counterfactuals in the years preceding 1642 and speculates as to how things might have worked out differently but did not. Such an effort is quite different from positing a counterfactual at the beginning (Hitler does not invade the USSR) and then imagining a whole new history that would have followed as the effect of that cause.

Whereas the virtual historian is forced to move ever further into the imaginary, the speculations of the restrained counterfactualist are pinned down by what actually did happen in the end. In imagining how things might have been different, the restrained counterfactualist tries to understand better what actually did happen. The restrained counterfactualist moves from known effect to hypothesized cause; the virtual historian exuberantly moves from the invisible (but supposed) cause to an effect that never actually happened. The restrained counterfactualist moves from the bottom up, from known evidence to a theory as to why it happened that way; the virtual historian moves from the top down, deducing a hypothetical effect from a speculative theory concerning how the world functions. The less likely the virtual historian is to have thought seriously about this theory, the more likely it is that he will hold it to be indubitable truth.

In his introduction to *Virtual History* Ferguson spends much effort trying to show that counterfactual history amounts to an attack on historical determinism (most notably, on the determinism allegedly promoted by Marxists). According to Ferguson, counterfactual history highlights the possibility of human agency in history. According to Richard Evans, we need to pay more attention than Ferguson does to underlying structural determinants. But both historians are surely focusing on the wrong issue, for the question "Human beings: do they have freedom or not?" is not a historian's question. Historians can offer no more than stale banalities on it because their disciplinary project already *assumes* a position, itself a banality, namely that human beings are both determined and free, both subordinate to external forces and capable of creating and exploiting such forces, both matter and spirit, both beasts and angels. No genuine determinist could ever be a true historian: such a person should rather study neurochemical, physical, or other forces. The same is true of anyone who believes that human beings soar above their circumstances like transcendental meditators: such a person will never be found contending with the archival muck that historians so avidly explore.

In fact, the fundamental point at issue in the matter of counterfactual history is the character of historical explanation. (Both Evans and Ferguson see this, but in their eagerness to joust with political opponents—allegedly deterministic leftists on the one hand, the "New Right" on the other—they tend to bury the point.) I mean by an *explanation* an attempt to say why something is the case (why it exists or existed, why it happened). One can equally well say that an explanation is an attempt to answer the question, "What causes (or caused) E?" This second wording raises a difficulty, since even at this late date many people—including many historians—adhere to a "regularity" view of causation, according to which our saying that C is the cause of E needs to involve a "constant conjunction" (Hume's term) of some sort connecting C and E. Reacting against the "regularity" view, R. G. Collingwood claimed in *The Idea of History* that historians do not (or at least should not) invoke causes. Rather, historians' explanations, Collingwood contended, are a matter of telling a story: the historian says that this happened and this happened and this happened, and from the story an explanation arises. In Collingwood's formulation, "when the historian has ascertained the facts, there is no further process of inquiring into their causes."[3] And although Collingwood does not discuss the matter explicitly, his argument in *The Idea of History* strongly implies a rejection of counterfactuality.[4]

As Carl Hempel showed with brilliant clarity in his 1942 paper, "The Function of General Laws in History," historians cannot offer explanations that conform to the regularity view.[5] Without going into the complexities of the discussion that followed the publication of Hempel's paper, let me simply assert that the only view of explanation that works for historians is one that focuses on counterfactuality and that allows the regularity criterion to recede into the background. For historians *in principle* cannot subsume their explanations under regularities: Hempel was right about this. Rather, when a historian suggests that, such as, "imperialism caused [or helped cause] World War I," he is *really* saying—if saying anything intelligent at all—something like "all other things being equal, if there had been no imperialism, there would have been no World War I." Of course, the historian is probably also saying more than this, for history is a field where multiple causes, at different levels, are assumed to operate. Thus the counterfactual reasoning that the historian deploys must be quite complex.

In the final section of his 1940 book, *An Essay on Metaphysics,* Collingwood himself offered a pragmatically oriented account of causation, one that has a strongly counterfactual resonance, for he suggests that what we can most readily imagine as *otherwise* in the situation that actually existed, we tend to promote to the status of a cause. Thus we tend to take as "the" cause of, say, a car accident whatever we, from our own particular perspective, can most readily imagine as something that could have been different. Think how many *possible* causes there might be: the faulty camber of the road, the too-high speed limit, the driver's carelessness in driving so fast, the driver's drinking, the flawed design of the car. Imagining away one or another element, we imagine the accident not happening—which thus establishes that element's causal character. This is a promising line of thinking that Collingwood conspicuously did not pursue in *The Idea of History.*[6]

The fact is, historians *must* engage in counterfactual reasoning. I note with dismay that I have encountered, more often than I would have liked, historians to whom this fact appears to be news. But perhaps this is not so surprising. If a historian sees his or her project as primarily one of describing or interpreting some past historical reality and is not interested in exploring causal relations, there would be no need for counterfactuals used for explanatory purposes. Some famous historians in the tradition of the French *Annales* school tradition were of this sort, much more interested in description and in suggestive juxtapositions than in causal analysis. The same tends to be true of the most recently dominant historiographical "paradigm," cultural history. One result is that when historians operating in these frameworks *do* try to make causal claims, they sometimes fail completely to understand what kind of reasoning is required to underpin such claims. Likewise, historians who maintain a deep commitment to some particular theory of history (such as, doctrinaire historical materialism and especially "dialectical materialism") will also be inclined to bypass counterfactuals: here, the theory tells them that what did happen pretty much *had* to happen. Nor does it seem likely that historians who see themselves as "just telling a story" will normally be inclined to think about how the story might have proceeded differently. In short, large numbers of historians have avoided all confrontation with counterfactual reasoning. Some of them, because of other, better aspects of their work, have been quite distinguished. We should therefore be grateful to the new counterfactualists for forcing us to think about the important role of counterfactuality in history.

NOTES

1. Niall Ferguson, ed., *Virtual History: Alternatives and Counterfactuals* (London: Picador, 1997; New York: Basic Books, 1999).

2. Various reviewers discuss *Axis and Allies* at http://www.amazon.com: search "Axis & Allies" (accessed September 2003).

3. R. G. Collingwood, *The Idea of History, with Lectures 1926–1928,* rev. ed., ed. Jan van der Dussen (Oxford, U.K.: Oxford University Press, 1994), 214.

4. See Collingwood, *Idea,* 246, in which he declares, "There is only one historical world" and rejects the relevance of "imaginary worlds" to history. Ferguson correctly notes in his introduction to *Virtual History* that the "idealist position" of Collingwood and Oakeshott "ruled out counterfactualism" (50).

5. Carl G. Hempel, "The Function of General Laws in History," in *Theories of History,* ed. Patrick Gardiner (Glencoe, Ill.: Free Press, 1960), 344–56.

6. R. G. Collingwood, *An Essay on Metaphysics* (Oxford, U.K.: Oxford University Press, 1940), 296–312, especially 304ff. The car-accident example appears in Collingwood's chapter "Causation in Practical Natural Science," not in his disappointing chapter "Causation in History."

Alternate History and Memory

Gavriel Rosenfeld

W hat would the field of alternate history do without its opponents? Since its recent emergence into the Western cultural and intellectual mainstream in the last generation, alternate history has garnered increasing attention in no small part due to the enduring opposition to it among many skeptical historians. By giving rise to controversy and sparking discussions, the critics of alternate history have ended up further contributing to the field's prominence. For this reason it is safe to say that without its opponents, the field of alternate history—to paraphrase Jean-Paul Sartre's flawed observations about anti-Semites' views of Jews—would have to invent them.

Fortunately, Richard Evans has spared the supporters of alternate history this demanding task by entering the fray with a long list of objections to the field. Evans raises important points in his eloquent critique of alternate history and scores a number of hits. But his overly narrow conception of the field ultimately ends up weakening the strength of his analysis.

Evans's complaint against alternate history is largely political in nature. He criticizes alternate history by identifying many of its leading practitioners as members of what he calls the "young fogey school" of conservative British historians, such as Niall Ferguson and Andrew Roberts. Evans describes these historians as embracing alternate history (and its attendant valorization of chance and contingency) as part of a broader conservative assault on the tradition of historical determinism long associated with Marxist historiography. This is a valid point that Evans augments with a convincing discussion of how conservatives have misunderstood the true nature of determinism in

From *Historically Speaking* 5 (March 2004)

traditional Western historiography. Yet no matter how valid his lengthy discussion of determinism may be, Evans himself exhibits signs of deterministic thinking when he effectively equates alternate history with conservative political thinking, asserting *"it is no accident* (emphasis added) . . . that so many proponents [of it] . . . have been located on the right wing of the political spectrum." Evans is correct that many conservatives have embraced alternate history; and he is convincing in showing, for example, how Niall Ferguson's speculative account of British neutrality in World War I expresses a clear conservative fantasy (in Ferguson's piece, Germany wins the Great War, thus preventing the eruption of World War II and allowing Britain to preserve its empire). Yet Evans goes too far in dismissing counterfactual history as "in the end little more than a rather obvious form of wishful thinking." Here, he seems ready to throw out the allohistorical baby because conservatives allegedly poured in the bathwater.

In fact, a broader survey of postwar alternate history reveals that it is far more complex in its political valences. Numerous examples could be cited, but alternate histories on the subject of the Nazis winning World War II provide an excellent example of demonstrating alternate history's compatibility with numerous political agendas. Since 1945 in England the scenario of the Nazis invading, defeating, and occupying Great Britain has been explored in an exceptionally large number of novels, short stories, plays, films, television programs, and speculative essays. Some have, indeed, been conservative in their political motivations. Early postwar accounts, such as Noel Coward's 1947 play, *Peace in Our Time,* or John W. Wall's novel *The Sound of His Horn* (both of which portray the Nazis as demonic beasts and the British as heroic resisters), for example, were clearly motivated by the conservative and highly patriotic agenda of triumphally validating the notion that Britain's historical decision to fight on against Nazi Germany in 1940 constituted the nation's "finest hour."

Yet from the mid-1960s through the late 1970s—to cite merely one of several important phases of significant postwar allohistorical productivity—British alternate histories increasingly began to dissolve the once-clear divisions between heroic Britons and demonic Germans by de-heroizing the former and de-demonizing the latter. Many works during these years portrayed the British collaborating with the Germans in occupied England, such as playwright Giles Cooper's 1964 television drama, *The Other Man* (starring Michael Caine as a collaborationist military officer overseeing a forced-labor brigade in Nazi-ruled India); Kevin Brownlow and Andrew Mollo's controversial 1964 film, *It Happened Here* (which portrays a collaborationist female medic in Nazi-occupied England); playwright Philip Mackie's 1978 BBC2 television miniseries, *An Englishman's Castle* (on the collaborationist British television industry's manipulation of public opinion); and novelist Len Deighton's 1978 bestseller, *SS-GB* (on collaborationist British police detectives working with the Nazi occupiers). Notably most of these writers stood on the left wing of the political spectrum and intended their works to critique the British status quo of the time. By the mid-1960s a highly pessimistic mood had developed within British society, rooted in the nation's increasingly obvious decline from great power status (typified by the loss of overseas colonies) and its general economic stagnation. In many ways the alternate histories of this downcast era represented a left-wing challenge to the self-satisfied myth of the "finest hour" so beloved by conservatives.

Many other examples could be cited to illustrate how liberals, not just conservatives, have utilized alternate history for political purposes. But there is another claim made by Evans that also needs to be questioned. Near the end of his essay, Evans flatly observes that alternate history, in promoting a subjective kind of wishful thinking, "contributes nothing to our understanding of what actually did happen" in the past. This is certainly true as far as it goes. But, of course, the task of history is not merely to explain what happened. In the last two decades, historians of memory have convincingly argued that another important task of historical scholarship is to explain how the events of the past have been perceived in collective consciousness. Alternate history may not reveal the reasons why history unfolded as it did, but it can certainly shed light on how it has been remembered.

Here again, British allohistorical accounts of a Nazi victory in World War II are significant for revealing the changing ways in which Britons have remembered the war experience. If early postwar accounts portrayed the Nazis as evil villains and the British as virtuous victims, the blurring of the line between the two in accounts since the mid-1960s reflects the gradual normalization of memory. As the Nazi experience has faded into the past, the emergence of new postwar generations and the onset of new postwar concerns have contributed to the fading horror of a Nazi wartime victory in British consciousness. Again, numerous other examples could be mentioned of other allohistorical themes that have been portrayed in other national contexts, but to repeat the obvious: alternate histories have immense value as sources enabling historians to chart the evolution of memory. Accounts of what never happened, in short, help us understand the memory of what did.

Finally, Evans's closing observations about the superiority of traditional history to alternate history can be questioned as well. Evans ends his essay by claiming that alternate history, far from liberating history from determinism, ends up "confining it in another that is more constricting" by allegedly prescribing an inevitable progression of events from a given point of divergence from the real historical record (that is, a lost battle being won, a major political leader dying prematurely, and so forth). He thus concludes that because alternate history "removes chance and contingency from history," it disqualifies itself from serious consideration as a tool of historical analysis. "History in the end," he asserts, "is and can only really be about finding out what happened . . . and understanding and explaining it, not positing alternative courses of development or indulging in bouts of wishful thinking."

Several things are flawed about this conclusion. Not only is it unnecessarily restrictive in its definition of the proper task of historical analysis, it is also based on an overly charitable view of the diverse motives that guide conventional historians in the first place. When Evans seeks to dismiss alternate history as the politically motivated tool of conservative daydreamers, he implies that traditional historiography is more objective and less beholden to political agendas. To be sure, most historians strive for objectivity by following commonly agreed-upon rules governing the use of evidence and the like. But in the last generation the profession has come to realize that the task of writing entails both a substantial degree of interpretation and various strategies of representation which are no less insulated from present day agendas, political or otherwise, than alternate history. One can see this in the traditional historical works of scholars who are also active practitioners of alternate history. To name merely one example, Niall Ferguson's traditional work of history, *The Pity of War,* contains many counterfactual observations that echo his larger theses about Britain's failure to remain neutral during World War I. It is not only conservatives, though, who have pursued political agendas in their work. A long and distinguished list of left-wing historians have been no less politically motivated in their own scholarship. To put it simply, traditional history is no less immune to potential politicization than alternate history.

In the end, of course, Evans is correct that traditional history will always remain superior in terms of explaining the past. But alternate history has its own contributions to make to the broader cause of historical understanding. Historians have yet to awaken to the potential of alternate history to shed light on historical memory. By beginning to write the history of alternate history and subjecting it to detailed empirical analysis, scholars will gradually begin to appreciate its significance as an important field of intellectual inquiry and cultural expression.

Counterfactualism Defended

Jeremy Black

One of the great pleasures of being a "nuts and bolts" historian is that every so often one's intellectual betters explain what I'm doing. Molière phrased it better, but it is late. Reading Richard Evans's characteristically thoughtful and interesting piece, I discover that, on at least one occasion, I've been "liberal whiggish" or "conservative, pessimistic," if not a "young fogey." For, I must confess, I have employed counterfactuals in *From Louis XIV to Napoleon: The Fate of a Great Power* (UCL, 1999), published an essay entitled "A Different West? Counterfactualism and the Rise of Britain to Great Power Status" (*Francia* 28/2 [2001]: 129–45), frequently lecture in the United States on the topic "Could the British Have Won the American War of Independence" (not "should"—more interesting, but outside my competence), and have discussed, on radio and in print, the "what if" the Jacobites had marched on from Derby in December 1745. I hope I can reassure Evans that I have no particular sympathy for Jacobites or any other defeated group, nor would I like the French to have beaten the British in their struggle for dominance in 1689–1815. Instead, my interest comes from the material I work on. The history of diplomacy, war, and government is not "very narrow" or only "about events," and it includes "processes, structures, cultures, societies, economies, and so on." The subjects are sometimes, indeed, approached in schematic and structural terms, a method I have contested, for it is difficult to spend a long time reading in the documents without being returned to their sense of uncertainty. Furthermore, it is necessary to probe this uncertainty in order to understand contemporary debates and to make evaluations

From *Historically Speaking* 5 (March 2004)

about competence. I have written a monograph on foreign policy and Parliament in the eighteenth century in which I try to evaluate the role of Parliament and to consider the quality of parliamentary debates. The former does rather require considering what would have happened had the role of Parliament been less prominent (let alone such counterfactuals as: would the Ochakov crisis of 1791 have been handled differently had Parliament not been in session—see, for example, the Dutch crisis of 1787?), while, in order to assess speeches, it is necessary to consider the practicality of the policies that were suggested.

Taking a different approach, given the apparent role of counterfactuals in modern politics, it is appropriate to ask why they should not be used to pose questions for historical research. Leaving aside the wonders of democracy in Florida and California, to take Britain in recent decades, the striking coal miners might have failed against Heath in 1974 but succeeded against Thatcher a decade later. Had there been no means of exploiting natural gas or oil in the North Sea, their absence would have put great pressure on Thatcherite public finances, making it harder to cut taxes and thus expand the private sector. It is instructive to contrast Britain with the majority of European states, which lacked these resources. Alternatively, earlier exploitation of the oil might have weakened the position of the coal industry (as well as removing the need to invest in nuclear power) and also possibly saved the reputation of the Wilson government by permitting it to avoid devaluation in 1967 or even enabled Heath to see off the miners' strikes. The ability of the Thatcher government in early 1985 to say that thanks to the state of electricity supplies there would be no power cuts helped speed the demise of the miners' strike. Again, by calling a general election in 1978, as he was pressed to do, Callaghan might have thwarted Thatcher; while, by not invading the Falklands in 1982, the course followed by previous juntas, the Argentinian military might have denied Thatcher the opportunity to regain the domestic political initiative. She might have been killed by the IRA, either at Brighton in 1984 or elsewhere. By failing to replace Thatcher in 1990 the Conservatives might have helped Labor to victory two years later and left them to bear the burden of the 1990s recession and the Maastricht debate, helping the Conservatives to return to power in 1997, if not earlier—a counterfactual that politicians have discussed with me and that clearly shapes part of their thinking. By refusing to support the U.S. in its war with Iraq in 2003, Blair would have faced a very different international situation, and this might have affected the domestic political debate about relations within Europe. The sum of these "what ifs" is that these processes are fragile and largely involve luck and circumstances. They also point out the extent to which events hang on circumstance. For example, the militancy of the petrol dispute in 2000, which momentarily posed the most serious public order crisis the Blair governments have faced, owed much to the extent to which farmers had been badly and recently affected by events. A number of the leaders of the blockades of the petrol depots were hauliers with farms who seemed doubly hit.

The electoral system could also have been changed, as the parties of the center—Liberals, Social Democrats, and, later, Liberal Democrats—demanded, producing the "realignment of British politics" pressed for in the SDP's founding Limehouse Declaration in 1981. Labor's failure in the Euro-elections in 1999, the first national election in Britain under a system of proportional representation, led the Labor government to abandon its commitment to holding a referendum on proportional representation before the next general election. Had such a system been introduced then, or earlier, as the Liberals and Liberal Democrats pressed for as the price of their support, it is likely that all governments would have been coalitions and probable, therefore, that centrist tendencies would have been dominant. This would have dramatically changed the history both of the individual political parties and the political history of the country itself.

The wider impact of such a "high political" change is less clear. There might have been, as is normal with proportional representation (PR) systems, a fragmentation of political parties, as well as an entry into mainstream politics of hitherto marginal groups that would have given political extremists, such as, the British National Party and ethnic groups, a particular voice. The impact of PR or, for that matter, the existing electoral system, on social and economic developments is less clear.

Such counterfactuals are not idle speculation. At any one moment, various developments seemed possible to people in the past, and the sole guarantee was that what was going to happen was not known. Contingency can also be extended to aspects of history that are not usually tackled through the "what if" approach. It is possible to consider different developments in public culture, arising, for example, from policies toward media regulation. In the case of the environment and transport, the consequences of more stringent restrictions on building on greenfield sites and of heavier fuel prices invite consideration. This is not idle. Such options play a major role in economic modelling and social planning.

To turn back from the present, comparative history also encourages a measure of counterfactualism. For example, the comparison of Chinese and Christian European government leads to the question of whether a particular type of state structure was necessary for the modernization seen in the West, an issue probed in recent scholarship. The Europeans might have possessed a system comparable to that in China had the fusion of church and state developed differently, but a widespread disengagement of the church and clergy from state government took place in the early modern period. By fostering the impact of ideological goals on commercial practices and aspirations, such a fusion of church and state might well have limited economic growth in Europe.

The pedagogical value of counterfactual approaches, handled carefully, was driven home to me when, at the age of fourteen, we played the Congress of Vienna at high school (I was given the nonvoting role of Talleyrand on the basis that I was the sole pupil who knew anything about the subject) and had to close with an essay explaining why our terms were different to those actually negotiated.

My research repeatedly underlines the extent of choice in foreign policy and the extent to which structural factors affected but did not determine these choices. This is linked to the issue of how far success and failure are inherent. It is reasonable to consider whether Louis XIV could have thwarted William III's plans in 1688 or whether greater effort could have sustained and strengthened the promising French positions in India and North America in the early 1750s. For geographical, cultural, and political reasons, France was different from Britain as an economy, a society, and a state, but these differences did not lead to inevitable consequences.

I suspect that, as active researchers, there are, in practice, no major differences between Richard Evans and myself but rather variations in emphasis that reflect our own specialties. Such pluralism is to be encouraged.

When Do Counterfactuals Work?

Robert Cowley

I would like to begin my remarks with two observations. Richard Evans has written a dismissal of counterfactual history that is at once learned and elegant, reasoned and reasonable. In not a few points, if by no means all, I find myself agreeing with him. But why hide my feelings? I am uneasy being set up as straw man in his essay, and I don't like being lumped, even by inference, with the New Right of history. The Right has never been my chosen refuge. Counterfactual history is not just the domain of conservatively inclined thinkers, as many of the contributors to this issue of *Historically Speaking* should testify.

Ideological pique aside, and it is mild at best, I should explain something that is relevant to this discussion. I wrote the introduction to *What If? 2* (or *More What If?* as it is called in the United Kingdom) with an American audience in mind. In this country our introduction to the study of history is rarely an enlightening experience. Below the college level, history is taught abominably, to an extent that most historians in the United Kingdom probably don't appreciate. The result is a nation of history illiterates. According to one recent survey—where do they get these facts?—when asked to pick from a list America's allies in World War II, more than half the high school seniors questioned named Italy, Germany, and Japan. "What is the significance of Memorial Day?" children touring Washington, D.C., were asked. The most frequent reply was "The day when the pools open."

From *Historically Speaking* 5 (March 2004)

Such answers can be easily multiplied, and the reason for them has to do with the way history is taught in this country. As I wrote, "We are force-fed history as social studies, an approach in which all races, nationalities, and sexes are given equal time: everyone must be included, no one can be offended. This surrender to special interests is not just distorting but boring." There is another unfortunate byproduct of the civics-cum-history approach, so deadening in its bland seriousness. Students—those few who have not already tuned out—are left with the impression that history is inevitable, that what happened could not have happened any other way. Where in their textbooks is the drama of clashing wills, motives, and ideas, of opposing economic and social forces, of accidents and contingencies?

By the time they reach college, most American students are ruined for history. Those fortunate to survive have a fair chance of encountering teachers who will, for the first time, make history exciting—unless, that is, they are not undone by the currently fashionable tyranny of race, gender, and ethnicity. But that is a matter I'd rather sidestep here.

Where does counterfactual history fit into this too often doleful picture? A central concern of legitimate historians it should never be. Still, it has earned a place considerably more elevated than E. H. Carr's "idle parlor game"—and even Carr, as Evans reminds us, allowed himself to imagine what would have happened in the Soviet Union if Lenin had survived into old age. Counterfactual speculations can help to awaken and nourish our historical imaginations. They can help as well to involve people in the historical process and to transform its examination from drudgery to entertainment in its best sense. That has been my aim in the three *What If?* books I've edited—that and the introduction of readers to some of the finest historians writing today.

History is properly the literature of what did happen, but that should not diminish the need for counterfactual speculation. It can be just as important to understand what did not happen as what did. A rigorous counterfactual examination has a way of making the stakes of a confrontation or a decision stand out in relief, to reveal their potentially abiding consequences. Too, it can focus on moments that were true turning points.

Let me give an example from military history, which is my particular field of authority. A counterfactual scenario helps to pick out the moment when, at the Battle of Gettysburg, the advantage passed from Robert E. Lee's Confederate invaders to the Union defenders strung out along Cemetery Ridge. Over the years Pickett's charge on the final afternoon may have gotten most of the attention; but climactic moments and turning points are not always the same thing. What if, on the second day of the battle, Colonel Joshua L.

Chamberlain and his Twentieth Maine Regiment had not been able to hold the rocky eminence known as Little Round Top? When his men ran out of ammunition, he ordered a bayonet charge against the Alabamians working their way up the hill. The charge succeeded. The battle may have turned on Chamberlain's decision. Had the Confederates taken Little Round Top, their guns would have commanded Cemetery Ridge, and the Union army would have been forced to retreat. Pickett's charge might never have taken place. Lee might have won his greatest victory.

Counterfactual scenarios have another important function. They can eliminate what has been called "hindsight bias"—an apt phrase that I first heard some years ago from Richard Ned Lebow at a conference on counterfactual history at Ohio State University. For example, when the German air offensive that we know as the Battle of Britain failed in the summer of 1940, could Hitler have still prevailed in Europe? Put that way, the question may sound almost preposterous. But for the past fifty-odd years, historians have persisted in asserting that he reached his high-water mark that early. Perhaps. Here is a place where counterfactual questions can show that history wasn't quite that simple—or should we say, undevious? What if Hitler had delayed his attack on the Soviet Union? What if, as John Keegan has suggested, he had instead leapfrogged from Greece into the Middle East? Or had sent Rommel more divisions in North Africa so that the Desert Fox could have overwhelmed the British and pushed on to Saudi Arabia, thus securing the oil Germany so desperately needed? There are other possibilities. In October 1941 Stalin could have fled Moscow for the Urals in the special train he had waiting, a panicky departure that might have signaled the crumbling of the Soviet armies. Operation Sledgehammer—the cross-Channel invasion of France that the Allies seriously contemplated in 1942—might have gone forward, with the same disastrous results of the Dieppe raid-in-force that August. The code breakers of Bletchley Park might not have cracked Ultra. The Germans might have thrown back the D-day invasion, Overlord. Since there was no follow-up operation planned, that would have prolonged the war by at least another year and—who knows?—led to the dropping of an atomic bomb on Berlin. What these "what ifs" tell us is that until the Allies forced Hitler into a two-front (three if one counts Italy) war in the summer of 1944, the war in Europe was very much in the balance.

Human options may be limitless, but in the confrontations of history, possible alternatives are ordinarily not. The reason is simple. Decisions are limited by the lack of imagination and aversion to risk taking of most decision makers. Politicians and generals tend not to be artists or madmen. Judgments, be they in a battle or a political campaign, do have to be made on the spot. Given time to reflect, however, decision makers tend to think in terms of counterfactual futures. What are war games, after all? The problem, as Evans wisely notes, is that events often do not turn out in quite the way counterfactualizing planners intended: witness our present predicament in Iraq. (One might argue, however, that those same planners may not have envisioned enough "what ifs.")

For all its potential usefulness, counterfactual history does have its liabilities. It should be regarded as a tool, nothing more. Evans has nicely summed up the objections to it. "What ifs" work best with matters military or political, less well with social, cultural, or economic history. For example, one might try to examine whether the depression of the 1930s in America would have been quite so severe had Calvin Coolidge ridden herd on the stock market in 1927 and 1928. He didn't, of course: regulation wasn't part of his philosophy of governing. More to the point, however, by the end of the 1920s (which for most people was anything but a "Jazz Age"), America was dealing with what T. S. Eliot called "vast impersonal forces"—to name just a few, overproduction, agricultural depression, the dislocations of too-rapid urbanization, and the fact that the vaunted prosperity of the decade had bypassed the majority of our population. Absent Coolidge, these are circumstances that hardly admit to the counterfactual.

Indeed, as Evans complains, counterfactual history does tend to focus too heavily on individuals. But even biographically weighted "what ifs" have their limitations. It's easy to enumerate the lucky breaks that propelled FDR to the presidency, as Geoffrey Ward has done in *What If? 2*. The luckiest of them all (both for him and for the United States) was his refusal to pose for newsreel cameramen a few moments longer when Giuseppe Zangara attempted to shoot him in Miami on February 15, 1933. What if the death of the president-elect—Zangara actually killed the mayor of Chicago, who was standing close by—had given us John Nance Garner, a man unequipped by desire or ability to guide the country through its worst crisis since the Civil War? Counterfactual speculation may help to explain why FDR got as far as he did. But it can never completely go inside his head to explain why this amiably shallow aristocrat became so unaccountably great.

Still, nothing should drive home the relevance—I started to say the poignance—of the counterfactual more than recent American history. What if those 537 Florida votes in the 2000 presidential election had gone the other way, as they might easily have done? What if the Supreme Court had declined to become involved or its 5-4 vote had gone in favor of a Florida recount? Or what if the FBI and the CIA had sniffed out a conspiracy before bin Laden's minions boarded those four airliners? Some of us might prefer to replace the "what ifs" with the judgmental "if only." We must resist the temptation. As Evans reminds us, wishful thinking is an unhistorical trap and one that we can do without.

Response

Richard J. Evans

Let's start by clearing away the rubbish. Most of it is in Edward Ingram's contribution, which attributes to me many views that I do not hold and devotes a lot of space to confused attacks on arguments I have never advanced. To begin at the beginning—and disregarding the cheap and rather puerile sarcasm which is evidently Ingram's stock-in-trade—I do not have a Manichean view of the world, whatever that is. I do not think that what happened is good: in my practice as a historian, I do not ascribe any moral qualities to what happened, but if I did, I would certainly not think that, for example, the deliberate murder of nearly six million Jews by the Nazis, something that undoubtedly did happen, was good. I have on many occasions written about the difficulty of ascertaining what happened in the past, though I persist in thinking that one can do it. A large part of the challenge of being a historian lies in this difficulty, but I do think that it often is possible to achieve certainty about what did happen and to distinguish it from what did not. Despite his claim that "what happened, we do not know and cannot find out," Ingram actually does seem pretty certain nonetheless that he himself can distinguish what happened from what didn't. Ingram's piece is littered with his own certainties about what happened, starting with "The Holocaust. It happened"— a statement made just a couple of lines after the one I've just quoted—and going on to Britain's declaration of war in 1914, Churchill's drinking champagne, and much more. So we're not really disagreeing there, then, though for some reason he clearly thinks we are.

From *Historically Speaking* 5 (March 2004)

Ingram's next section contains a whole series of confusions about contingency and determinacy. Contingency just means uncertainty (one uncertain event is dependent on the occurrence of another uncertain event and so on); determinism, though you'll find several different definitions of it in Niall Ferguson's introduction to his collection on *Virtual History*, usually means that things are caused by factors external to the human will. To put it another way, we can't be sure that things were bound to happen the way they did, but we can usually be sure that they did not happen just because someone wanted them to. At this point, Ingram brings in the example of a butterfly beating its wings in one place leading to a chain of chance events that cause a hurricane in another, an example I've never used in any of my work, though he claims I have. And he also brings in Carr's example of a car crash. Perhaps because he had spent two decades working as a civil servant before he turned to history, Carr thought that a car crash or some similar event should only be explained by the historian in terms that encouraged the prevention of car crashes in the future. Thus it was important to say a crash was caused by drunk driving but irrelevant to suggest it was caused by a chance event such as a butterfly distracting the driver's attention (though Carr did not in fact use this example). I've said on more than one occasion that Carr's elimination of chance from history in this way won't do; chances and accidents do happen, and historians have to take them into account when explaining things. But events also usually have larger structural determinants, which interact with chance to produce them; working out the precise mix is surely what most historians spend much of their time doing. And in doing this we cannot pay any attention to whether or not our explanations will be useful to anyone, otherwise major distortions will surely creep in, as indeed they did to Carr's own work on Soviet Russia.

As for the battle of Waterloo, I really can't see how imagining what might have happened had Napoleon won and not Wellington (and Blücher, because we have to remember that it was a German as well as a British victory) could possibly lead us to believe that victory is not a clear-cut phenomenon. Waterloo seems a pretty clear-cut victory to me. After it Napoleon was exiled to St. Helena and never came back; the French monarchy was restored; and the Vienna Peace Settlement was completed. France did not become a major European power again for another forty years. Similarly with the Holocaust. I fail to see why "to find out why, to whom, at what speed, and in what circumstances it happened, one has to state a series of counterfactual propositions," as Ingram claims. To find out all these things, surely, one has to undertake historical research, read contemporary documents, and consider eyewitness testimony, as historians have indeed been doing for many years now. Counterfactualism has nothing to do with it.

How Ingram imagines that events do not matter for me, as he claims in his next paragraph, is incomprehensible. Let me direct him to any of my books —*Lying about Hitler,* for example, or *The Coming of the Third Reich*—and he will see that they are jam-packed with accounts of events of all kinds, many of them occupying a pivotal place in the arguments I put forward. I'm not an *Annales* historian who thinks that events are insignificant in the larger scale of things. The Industrial Revolution, however, was not in the normal sense of the word an event, but, as Ingram correctly describes it, a process. The term *Industrial Revolution* has been questioned, but the things that made up the process—mechanical inventions, steam power, the growth of the iron and steel industry, and so on—have not. They happened, and the questions are, how do we link them together and how do we interpret the overall process of which they were a part? Ingram's confident statements of fact—that Britain was "on the sidelines, anchored in the *ancien régime*" by the mid-nineteenth century—are not statements of fact at all but controversial claims of interpretation that many would dispute. If anyone is using sleight of hand here, it's Ingram, who seeks to discredit the notion of a fact by using it to apply to interpretations.

Ingram goes on to territory where he is more at home when he turns to the origins of the First World War. Here he is confusing my criticism of Ferguson with an exposition of my own views. All I said was that if Ferguson wants to understand why Britain declared war in 1914, it is not necessary for him to go into an elaborate explanation of why the British cabinet was wrong to fear a German victory over France and Russia: it is surely enough to know that that fear was what impelled them to make the declaration of war. I did not say that that was what I thought the sole cause was; though if I did think that, then I would have to go on to ask why the British feared a German victory. And the answer then would lie in structural factors: the growth of German economic power, the threat to the British Empire from German *Weltpolitik,* the building of the German navy, the long-term British doctrine of the balance of power, and so on and so forth, so that my explanation would in no way be a simple one, as Ingram claims.

It may be rather simpleminded of me to say so, but I cannot see what is to be gained in terms of understanding the British decision to declare war in 1914 by imagining what might have happened had Britain not followed this up with military action or declared war on Russia instead. As for changing interpretations of the origins of the war in a more general sense, it's no more true to say that "the Germans changed their paradigm forty years ago" as a result of Fritz Fischer's work than it is to say that "the English . . . attribute the outbreak of war to the Central Powers' actions alone." Read either German or British historians on both points, and you will still find plenty of controversy and disagreement about them. If this is Ingram's way of making a "factual" statement, then I'm not very impressed, though I don't think it would be of much use to imagine what might have happened to historians' interpretations of the origins of the war had Fritz Fischer not written *Griff nach der Weltmacht*. After all, documents such as the September Programme were lying there in the archives waiting to be discovered, and if Fischer hadn't found them, somebody else eventually would have.

It's not worth wasting much time on Ingram's rather silly claims about later events causing earlier ones. What he really means is that the fact that we have experienced a whole series of events since the one we're trying to explain inevitably colors our explanation with hindsight, a point that of course I would accept. This brings us to 1940. I did not say that it was right for Britain to continue fighting Germany in 1940, merely that the counterfactual claim by Paul Addison that a separate Anglo-German peace in 1940 would eventually have led to the incorporation of Britain into a Nazi empire by a Germany greatly strengthened by victory over Russia is at least as plausible as the counterfactual claim by John Charmley that such a peace would have preserved the British Empire or for that matter the counterfactual claim by Andrew Roberts that the result would have been a Soviet Empire stretching from Vladivostok to Boulogne. Ingram's dismissal in a couple of sentences of the widely held view among historians that the main causes of the collapse of the British Empire were the rise of anticolonialism in the colonies and the rise of a rival, informal empire in the shape of the world hegemony of the United States and not the loss of resources spent by Britain in fighting the Second World War is unconvincing, to say the least.

Ingram says I object to the use of the term *foolish* to describe the British decision to fight Germany in 1939 and to continue doing so in 1940. But I'm not aware of anyone who has used it, still less have I raised any objections; my use of the word is entirely within Ingram's own imagination. Following David Irving, he claims that Churchill wanted to go on fighting because he was drunk a lot of the time and liked excitement. Presenting this as an innuendo ("leaves one wondering") rather than an opinion will not fool anyone. At least it is clear enough at this point what he thinks. But Ingram becomes confused once more when he appears to attribute to me the very views which I am criticizing in the counterfactual writing of the young conservative Euro-skeptic historians: "Perhaps for Englishmen of the age of Margaret Thatcher, who said that Britain had not won the Second World War in order that Germany should be reunited, the war never ends." "Why," Ingram asks, "should it provide the imaginative and emotional foundation for the lives of their children?" Well, quite: my question, too.

Similarly, it's not my treatment of Britain's role in the world wars that privileges intention over action but the treatment of the counterfactualists I'm criticizing. It's they who have drawn parallels between 1914 and 1940, not I. It's Niall Ferguson, not I, who insists that knowing what statesmen thought is the key to explaining why things happened. When Ingram says that "readers of histories want to know not only what contemporaries thought was happening but also what was," I can only applaud him, though I can't resist pointing out that this desire surely drives the historian to provide the very facts ("what was") that Ingram says are so impossible to find out anyway. It's precisely the point I'm trying to make that we can't restrict ourselves to what people thought, otherwise we'd never understand a phenomenon like the great witch-hunts of the early modern period. (How could we be satisfied with an explanation that reproduced the view of contemporaries that there were a lot of witch trials because there were a lot of witches about?) So I don't "doubtless approve" of historians who try to write a narrative solely from the perspective of participants, as if that were possible anyway.

Finally, of course, I agree that historical explanation demands the application of a theory, but Ingram's account of how to go about this is as confused as everything else in his essay. You apply a theory of the causes of serf revolts to find out why there was a serf revolt in one rural region in the thirteenth century but not in another, and that implies the counterfactual statement that if the conditions had been present in one area where no revolt occurred, then a revolt might have taken place there, too. But that's only really a secondary consideration. The historian's main activity is actually a positive one: it's to look at the conditions in areas where the serfs revolted to see if they had anything in common and, in the light of that research, to modify the theory of serf revolts if necessary and conclude that the serfs didn't revolt elsewhere because the conditions satisfying the theory weren't present. None of this really involves speculation on what might have happened as the historian's primary concern. And if, to conclude, as Ingram claims, political science teaches us that theories cannot be invalidated by evidence, then it's probably best to ignore it, though in practice, of course, political scientists are constantly trying to invalidate or modify theories by showing that they don't fit the evidence they purport to explain. So Ingram's claim is a false one here, too.

After all this it's a relief to turn to the thoughtful contribution by Richard Ned Lebow. Much of what he has to say one can only agree with. Econometric history has in the past made intelligent use of counterfactuals, most famously of course in Robert Fogel's work on the economic impact of railways in the United States. Similarly population history often gains from projecting peacetime trends and then assessing what difference a war made by measuring them against the real population statistics generated in wartime. There's nothing wrong with this. I've done something like it myself in trying to calculate the impact of disease in nineteenth-century Germany. Moreover, I wouldn't wish to deny that every causal explanation at least implies a counterfactual. What would have happened in Russia had Lenin lived on into the 1940s is a counterfactual of a rather larger sort. It seems to me that in the end counterfactuals such as these are only present in the background of historians' explanations; they're not really central to them. If we want to know whether Stalinism was the product of Stalin's personality or the structural outcome of the Bolshevik Revolution, we will expend most of our effort on looking at the personality of Stalin and the structure of Bolshevism, not on imagining what Lenin might have done, which is by definition unknowable. Similarly with the impact of nuclear weapons on international politics, mutatis mutandis. Some of Lebow's key examples in any case are not historical at all but policy related: affirmative action, free trade, European integration, and appeasement are policy issues where we put forward alternatives not as counterfactuals but as real possibilities for the future.

Lebow's point that counterfactuals often represent particular points of view is well taken; it's a point that's central to my own argument as well. The real problems arise, however, when historians' parti pris seduces them into imagining long-term alternative histories about which one can actually know nothing at all. Who is to say that had Germany won the First World War there would have been no Hitler (or someone very much like him) and no Holocaust? It depends on a whole host of unknowables: by how much and in what way Germany would have won the war, whether victory spurred on Germany's international ambitions, what the response would have been among the defeated Allies, and so on. Henry Ashby Turner Jr.'s speculation that an authoritarian military dictatorship in Germany in the 1930s would have avoided the Holocaust is unknowable, too, especially given the German military's long-term aim of conquering Eastern Europe and its deeprooted anti-Semitic prejudices. That depends in turn on what you think caused the Holocaust, something about which there are many different rival theories.

Another way of putting this is to say that we don't have much direct evidence about the motives of those who made the decision. But there is plenty of indirect evidence in various forms, starting with Hitler's numerous, extreme, and murderously phrased anti-Semitic speeches. We make inferences from this, from the situation in Europe and Germany in 1941, and from other kinds of evidence, too. Often such explanations, as Lebow says, are at a high level of abstraction, especially when we are dealing with large-scale phenomena like the rise and fall of empires. The higher the level of abstraction, the greater the amount of inference. Similarly, as Lebow says, with counterfactuals; and I've no quarrel with any of the points he makes here. So I look forward very much to the forthcoming book which he is editing with Geoffrey Parker, which on the evidence of his contribution to this debate promises to raise the practice of counterfactual history to a new level, something that's badly needed.[1]

William H. McNeill's contribution takes the line that I'm attacking examples of counterfactual history that are simply too silly to be taken seriously. Unfortunately, however, he is wrong in supposing that no one thinks that individuals operate on history without external constraints or that only the alternatives actually considered by contemporaries may be taken into account. There are historians around who do actually believe these things or at least have said they do. McNeill's characteristically sweeping and global ruminations focus on the unintended or unexpected results of human action and the limits of humankind's power to shape the future. His eloquent and moving plea for consensus as a basis for human action is well taken. But nothing of what he says has any direct relevance to counterfactuals, except to say that they can be sobering as well as amusing, two adjectives with which I would not wish to quarrel.

The contribution of Allan Megill, another historian, like McNeill, whose work I've read with admiration and profit over the years, makes a useful distinction between "restrained" and "exuberant" counterfactual history, the latter a parlor game, based on constructing alternative futures to what happened, the former a serious scholarly activity, based on constructing alternative pasts. Megill's demolition of the "exuberant" variety could hardly be bettered. In fact we have few points of disagreement here. I take Megill's point that the practice of history assumes that human beings are partly free and partly determined, which is what I tried to say myself; my quarrel with Ferguson is precisely that he's engaging in a false polarization of freedom and determination. I also take his point that explaining something by adducing a cause implies thinking about how things might have turned out differently had that cause not been present. I don't think many historians would in practice posit a regular, unchanging relationship between a cause and an effect—say, imperialism and world wars—since it's invariably falsified by the evidence. And the Collingwoodian exercise he suggests, of positing many possible causes for an event, with evidence available for the presence of all of them, then isolating the one that was most important by imagining whether it would have happened had the others not been present, is a useful one and one which, surely, historians engage in all the time, as Megill says. However, I don't see much discussion of this particular, very limited use of counterfactuals in the literature on counterfactuals more generally. Perhaps there should be.

One of the points which none of the contributors to this debate has so far addressed is the question of why counterfactual history has recently become so popular. I essayed a few brief explanations in my own piece: postmodern playfulness and insistence on the arbitrariness of knowledge, despair at the seeming uncontrollability of the world, the death of the great determinist ideologies, and so on. One of them, at least in Britain, is undoubtedly in my view the emergence of conservative hostility to the European Union, at least since 1989, which is a major reason, I believe, why so many of the counterfactualists have been on the right. Gavriel Rosenfeld's extremely knowledgeable and interesting real history of counterfactual imaginings of what might have happened had the Germans invaded and occupied Britain in 1940 persuasively charts the change from patriotic portrayals in the 1940s and 1950s to the self-doubt and pessimism of the 1970s and 1980s. One might add that the 1970s and 1980s saw a satirical puncturing of the patriotic myths of Britain in 1940, in programs drawing loosely on real history such as "Dad's Army." There are clear parallels here to British attitudes toward the Germans. By the end of this period these had become admiring rather than anything else, holding Germany up as a prosperous, efficient, hard-working, and well-ordered society whose characteristics were sadly lacking in a Britain visibly in decline.

One obvious difference between all these alternative histories and those of the last decade or so, however, has been that the current wave of alternative history is being spearheaded by real professional historians, unlike that of earlier decades, which was the province of film and television producers, novelists, and screenwriters. Another is that the tide has turned again in British views of the Germans, which have been overwhelmingly negative since 1989, equating Germans with Nazis and wallowing once more in the retrospective myths of 1940. The fading away of British portrayals of a Nazi-ruled society in 1940 was not a reflection of fading memory but of changing public images of Germany. There has been a massive revival of memory since 1990; no "gradual normalization of memory" has taken place, as Rosenfeld claims, rather the contrary. The reasons for this dramatic change are too complicated to go into here, but what does need to be said is that I'm writing in the context of the beginning of the twenty-first century, not the 1960s or 1970s. I don't mean to say that counterfactual history is always and inevitably conservative, just that in Britain, it is at the moment.

One cannot disagree, therefore, with Rosenfeld's claim that the real history of counterfactual histories provides important evidence for writing the real history of memory and culture. After all, in a way, that is what I've tried to do in my attempt to explain why counterfactual history has become popular in Britain in the last few years. But, interesting though this is, it has nothing to do with the question of whether historians' use of real counterfactual history in the study of the real past is a good idea or not. Nor would I wish to disagree with Rosenfeld's observation that historians of all political hues are bound to link their historical work to their present-day concerns. If he inferred from my article that I thought real historiography was not political, then I certainly did not mean to imply it. What I did mean to imply, however, was that by liberating history from the constraints of evidence, counterfactual history, at least in its "exuberant" version, allows the political imagination to roam unfettered across the realm of might-have-beens, turning history into propaganda, while the political or social purpose of real history, as Rosenfeld says, is caught in a web of facts and so inevitably is diluted, sublimated, or even in some cases confounded by what the historian finds in the evidence; for historical evidence, unlike historical imagination, cannot be altered at will to make it conform to how one would like things to have been.

Jeremy Black, however, will not accept my contention that the question of what might have happened implies an agenda as to what should or should not have happened. In his own case this may well be right. For the speculations that fill his contribution to the debate are mostly of the rather inconsequential parlor-game variety. So what if Britain had not had North Sea oil in the 1980s? It is enough to know that Britain did have North Sea oil, if one is seeking to use this fact to help explain how Mrs. Thatcher's government managed to defeat the coalminers in 1984 whereas its absence had doomed her predecessor Mr. Heath in his attempt to defeat them a decade earlier. This is just another example of the causal explanation implying a counterfactual alternative (what would have happened if Britain had not had North Sea oil in 1984?) without the counterfactual actually being primary to the explanation. Black's speculations on what might have happened had Mrs. Thatcher continued in power after 1990 are all very amusing, and some of the factors he mentions might well have played a role in turning her ministers against her at the time (they clearly considered her an electoral liability by that stage, as well as redundant in other ways, too), but do they really help explain what happened in the end?

And, of course, in the usual way, one can posit equally plausible alternatives to Black's counterfactuals. One wonders, for example, whether proportional representation would have made that much difference to British governments and political parties, since all the parties are fighting over the center ground of politics anyway, even including the Conservatives after the replacement of Iain Duncan Smith as leader by the more politically astute Michael Howard, if one is to believe him. Black's examples reinforce my view that the modern British historians who engage in counterfactual speculations do so from the vantage point of a narrowly conceived history of kings and battles, high politics and diplomacy, so it is refreshing to see Black engaging in speculation as to what might have happened to modernization had Europe had state structures like those of China in the early modern period. Still, here too, the onus lies on the historian to show how European state structures helped modernization and Chinese hindered it, and in this process speculating on what might have happened had things been the other way round does not really seem to help much. Finally, in much of what he writes, like Lebow, Black considers counterfactual speculation more as a factor influencing policy decisions than as a factor in enabling historical understanding, which is all well and good but does not have a lot to do with the questions under discussion here.

Finally, since I don't know Robert Cowley at all, I obviously owe him an apology for lumping him with the New Right of history if he does not want to be lumped in this way. However, his repeated complaints about "the currently fashionable tyranny of race, gender, and ethnicity" would seem to place him somewhere on the Right if I know anything at all about the American political scene. As far as I'm concerned, the more about race, gender, and ethnicity in history, the better. Where I can agree with him is when he declares that "a rigorous counterfactual examination has a way of making the stakes of a confrontation or a decision stand out in relief." The key word here is "rigorous," and once more we're back to "the principle of minimal rewrite," as Philip Tetlock puts it, a principle in which we can surely all concur. But its uses remain in my view strictly limited. So what if Pickett had not charged at the Battle of Gettysburg or Chamberlain lost the Little Round Top? Surely there were larger determining factors that weighed decisively in the scales of victory and defeat in the Civil War? It's fun to think what might have happened had Hitler not attacked the Soviet Union in 1941, but the real challenge lies in explaining why he did.

Cowley graciously concedes my charges that as currently practiced, counterfactual history works best with military and political history and focuses too heavily on individuals, and he agrees that we can do without wishful thinking. My point, however, is that counterfactual history encourages these things—a narrowly traditional view of history and a degree of wishful thinking that is distorting, to say the least. As the numerous examples cited in the present discussion show, it need not be that way. Counterfactual history is just a tool of historical analysis, as Cowley says, and has to be used with caution. It has to be applied in very specific, carefully delimited contexts if it is applied at all, and we have to be aware of its limitations, which are extremely severe. It's hard enough finding out what was, let alone reaching any kind of tenable conclusions on what wasn't. But if counterfactual history didn't exist, then the world of historical debate would surely be a poorer place. In his concluding contribution, Robert Cowley lets slip the fact that he has edited three volumes of *What If?* In my ignorance, I thought there were only two. I'm off to buy the third one right away.

NOTE

1. Philip Tetlock, Richard Ned Lebow, and Geoffrey Parker, eds., *Unmaking the West: "What-If?" Scenarios That Rewrite World History* (Ann Arbor: University of Michigan Press, 2006).

Further Readings

Historical Thinking, Theory, and the Philosophy of History

Ankersmit, Frank, and Hans Kellner, eds. *A New Philosophy of History.* Chicago: University of Chicago Press, 1995.

Appleby, Joyce, Lynn Hunt, and Margaret Jacobs. *Telling the Truth about History.* New York: Norton, 1994.

Berkhofer, Robert F. Jr. *Beyond the Great Story: History as Text and Discourse.* Cambridge, Mass.: Harvard/Belknap, 1995.

Breisach, Ernst. *Historiography: Ancient, Medieval, and Modern.* 2nd ed. Chicago: University of Chicago Press, 1983. 1994.

Burns, Robert, and Hugh Rayment-Pickard, eds. *Philosophies of History: From Enlightenment to Postmodernity.* Oxford: Blackwell, 2000.

Charkrabarty, Dipesh. *Provincializing Europe: Postcolonial Thought and Historical Difference.* Princeton, N.J.: Princeton University Press, 2000.

Clark, Elizabeth A. *History, Theory, Text: Historians and the Linguistic Turn.* Cambridge, Mass.: Harvard University Press, 2004.

Collingwood, R. G. *The Idea of History.* Rev. ed. Oxford: Oxford University Press, 1993.

Domańska, Ewa. *Encounters: Philosophy of History after Postmodernism.* Charlottesville: University Press of Virginia, 1998.

Fasolt, Constantin. *The Limits of History.* Chicago: University of Chicago Press, 2004.

Fulbrook, Mary. *Historical Theory.* London: Routledge, 2002.

Haskell, Thomas L. *Objectivity Is Not Neutrality: Explanatory Schemes in History.* Baltimore: Johns Hopkins University Press, 1998.

Jenkins, Keith. *Re-Thinking History.* London: Routledge, 1991.

———. *Why History? Ethics and Postmodernity.* London: Routledge, 1999.

Kramer, Lloyd, and Sarah Maza, eds. *A Companion to Western Historical Thought.* Oxford: Blackwell, 2002.

Lemon, M. C. *Philosophy of History: A Guide for Students.* London: Routledge, 2003.

Lowenthal, David. *The Past Is a Foreign Country.* Cambridge, U.K.: Cambridge University Press, 1985.

Lukacs, John. *Historical Consciousness: The Remembered Past.* New York: Harper & Row, 1968.

———. *At the End of an Age.* New Haven, Conn.: Yale University Press, 2002.

McCullagh, C. Behan. *The Logic of History: Putting Postmodernism in Perspective.* London: Routledge, 2003.

———. *The Truth of History.* London: Routledge, 1998.

Munslow, Alun. *Deconstructing History.* London: Routledge, 1997.

———. *The New History.* Harlow, U.K.: Pearson Longman, 2003.

———, ed. *The Routledge Companion to Historical Studies.* London: Routledge, 2000.

Rüsen, Jörn, ed. *Western Historical Thinking: An Intercultural Debate.* New York: Berghahn, 2002.

Seixas, Peter, ed. *Theorizing Historical Consciousness.* Toronto: University of Toronto Press, 2004.

Southgate, Beverley. *History: What and Why? Ancient, Modern, and Postmodern Perspectives.* London: Routledge, 1996.

———. *Postmodernism in History: Fear or Freedom?* London: Routledge, 2003.

———. *Why Bother with History? Ancient, Modern, and Postmodern Motivations.* Harlow, U.K.: Longman, 2000.

Stanford, Michael. *An Introduction to the Philosophy of History.* Oxford: Blackwell, 1998.

Thompson, Willie. *Postmodernism and History.* Houndmills, Basingstoke, U.K.: Palgrave Macmillan, 2004.

Veyne, Paul. *Writing History.* Translated by Mina Moore-Rinvolucri. Middleton, Conn.: Wesleyan University Press, 1971, 1984.

Historical Method and Practice, Historiography

Bentley, Michael. *Modern Historiography: An Introduction.* London: Routledge, 1999.

Black, Jeremy. *Using History.* London: Hodder Arnold, 2005.

Carr, Edward Hallett. *What Is History?* New York: Vintage, 1961.

Elton, G. R. *The Practice of History.* 2nd ed. Oxford: Blackwell, 2002. With an afterword by Richard J. Evans.

Cannadine, David, ed. *What Is History Now?* Houndmills, Basingstoke, U.K.: Palgrave Macmillan, 2002.

Evans, Richard J. *In Defense of History.* New York: Norton, 1999.

Fox-Genovese, Elizabeth, and Elisabeth Lasch-Quinn, eds. *Reconstructing History: The Emergence of a New Historical Society.* London: Routledge, 1999.

Fuchs, Eckhardt, and Benedikt Stuchtey. *Across Cultural Borders: Historiography in Global Perspective.* Lanham, Md.: Rowman & Littlefield, 2002.

Gaddis, John Lewis. *The Landscape of History: How Historians Map the Past.* Oxford, U.K.: Oxford University Press, 2002.

Henige, David. *Historical Evidence and Argument.* Madison: University of Wisconsin Press, 2005.

Howell, Martha, and Walter Prevenier. *From Reliable Sources: An Introduction to Historical Methods.* Ithaca, N.Y.: Cornell University Press, 2001.

Iggers, Georg G. *Historiography in the Twentieth Century: From Scientific Objectivity to the Postmodern Challenge.* Hanover, N.H.: Wesleyan University Press, 1997.

Marwick, Arthur. *The New Nature of History: Knowledge, Evidence, Language.* Houndsmill, Basingstoke, U.K.: Palgrave, 2001.

Megill, Allan. *Historical Knowledge, Historical Error: A Contemporary Guide to Practice.* Chicago: University of Chicago Press, 2007.

Novick, Peter. *That Noble Dream: The "Objectivity Question" and the American Historical Profession.* Cambridge, U.K.: Cambridge University Press, 1988.

Tosh, John. *The Pursuit of History: Aims, Methods and New Directions in the Study of Modern History.* 2nd ed. London: Longman, 1994.

Vincent, John. *An Intelligent Person's Guide to History.* London: Duckworth Overlook, 1996, 2006.

Wang, Q. Edward, and Franz L. Fillafer, eds. *The Many Faces of Clio: Cross-cultural Approaches to Historiography.* New York: Berhahn Books, 2006.

Wineburg, Sam. *Historical Thinking and Other Unnatural Acts: Charting the Future of Teaching the Past.* Philadelphia: Temple University Press, 2001.

Counterfactuals

Cowley, Robert, ed. *What If? The World's Foremost Military Historians Imagine What Might Have Been.* New York: Berkley Books, 1999.

———. *What If? 2: Eminent Historians Imagine What Might Have Been.* New York: Berkley Books, 2001.

———. *What Ifs? of American History: Eminent Historians Imagine What Might Have Been.* New York: Berkley Books, 2003.

Ferguson, Niall, ed. *Virtual History: Alternatives and Counterfactuals.* New York: Basic, 1997.

Hawthorn, Geoffrey. *Plausible Worlds: Possibility and Understanding in History and the Social Sciences.* Cambridge, U.K.: Cambridge University Press, 1991.

Roberts, Andrew, ed., *What Ifs? Twelve Leading Historians Record What Might Have Been.* London: Weidenfeld and Nicolson, 2005.

Rosenfeld, Gavriel D. *The World Hitler Never Made: Alternate History and the Memory of Nazism.* Cambridge, U.K.: Cambridge University Press, 2005.

Tetlock, Philip, Richard Ned Lebow, and Geoffrey Parker, eds. *Unmaking the West: "What If" Scenarios That Rewrite World History.* Ann Arbor: University of Michigan Press, 2006.

Winik, Jay. *April 1865: The Month That Saved America.* New York: HarperCollins, 2001.

Contributors

JEREMY BLACK is professor of history at the University of Exeter. Among his scores of books are *The Hanoverians: The History of the Dynasty* (2004), *Using History* (2005), and *George III: America's Last King* (2006).

DAVID CANNADINE is Queen Elizabeth the Queen Mother Professor of British History at the Institute of Historical Research, University of London. He is the author of many books, including the prize-winning *The Decline and Fall of the British Aristocracy* (1990), *Ornamentalism: How the British Saw Their Empire* (2001), *Mellon: An American Life* (2006). He is editor of *What Is History Now?* (2004).

ROBERT COWLEY is the founding editor of *MHQ: The Quarterly Journal of Military History* and editor of the multivolume *What If?* series.

RICHARD J. EVANS is professor of modern history at Cambridge University. A specialist in German social and cultural history, Evans is also widely known for his historiographical writing, especially *In Defense of History* (1997). He wrote a new introduction to E. H. Carr's *What Is History?* (2001) and a new afterword to G. R. Elton's *Practice of History* (2001). He is currently working on a three-volume history of the Third Reich, of which the first two volumes, *The Coming of the Third Reich* (2004) and *The Third Reich in Power, 1933–1939* (2005), have been published.

EDWARD INGRAM is the founder and editor of *The International History Review*. His most recent works are *Empire-Building and Empire-Builders* (1995) and *The British Empire as a World Power* (2001).

RICHARD NED LEBOW is the James O. Freedman Presidential Professor of Government at Dartmouth College and fellow of the Centre of International Relations at the University of Cambridge. His *Tragic Vision of Politics: Ethics, Interests, and Orders* (2003) won the Alexander L. George Award for the best book in political psychology. His most recent book, coedited with Claudio Fogu and Wulf Kansteiner, is *The Politics of Memory in Postwar Europe* (2006).

JOSEPH S. LUCAS is editor of *Historically Speaking* and assistant director of the Historical Society. His articles have appeared in *Explorations in Early American Culture* and the *Journal of the Historical Society*.

JOHN LUKACS is an internationally read and praised historian, the author of more than twenty books, a winner of prizes, past president of the American Catholic

Historical Association, and member of the Royal Historical Society of the United Kingdom.

C. BEHAN McCULLAGH is a reader and associate professor in philosophy at La Trobe University. He is author of *The Truth of History* (1997) and *The Logic of History: Putting Postmodernism in Perspective* (2003).

WILLIAM H. McNEILL is the Robert A. Millikan Distinguished Service Professor of History Emeritus at the University of Chicago. His is widely considered the one of the most influential historians of the twentieth century, particularly for his seminal work in world history. His most recent book is *The Pursuit of Truth: A Historian's Memoir* (2005).

ALLAN MEGILL is professor of history at the University of Virginia. He is author of *Karl Marx: The Burden of Reason* (2002) and *Historical Knowledge, Historical Error: A Contemporary Guide to Practice* (2007) and editor of *Rethinking Objectivity* (1994).

GAVRIEL ROSENFELD is associate professor of German history at Fairfield University. He is author of *Munich and Memory* (2000) and *The World Hitler Never Made* (2005).

PETER SEIXAS is professor and Canada Research Chair in the Department of Curriculum Studies at the University of British Columbia. He is the founding director of the Centre for the Study of Historical Consciousness and is editor of *Theorizing Historical Consciousness* (2004).

BEVERLEY SOUTHGATE is reader emeritus in the history of ideas at the University of Hertfordshire. He is author of *History: What and Why?* (1996), *Why Bother with History?* (2000), *Postmodernism in History: Fear or Freedom?* (2003), and *What Is History For?* (2005).

WILLIE THOMPSON, formerly professor of contemporary history at Glasgow Caledonian University, is visiting professor at the University of Northumbria at Newcastle-upon-Tyne. He is author of *What Happened to History?* (2000) and *Postmodernism and History* (2003).

SAM WINEBURG is professor of education and chair, Department of Curriculum and Teacher Education, and professor of history (by courtesy) at Stanford University. He is author of the award-winning *Historical Thinking and Other Unnatural Acts: Charting the Future of Teaching the Past* (2001).

DONALD A. YERXA is editor of *Historically Speaking* and professor of history at Eastern Nazarene College. He is the author of three books, including *Admirals and Empire* (1991) and with Karl W. Giberson *Species of Origins* (2002). He has interviewed numerous historians and scholars for several publications.

Index